KARO Recipes from the Sweet Past to the Delicious Present

Over 200 ways
to use Karo® Corn Syrup
in all your cooking.

1904

1911

1917

1921

1937

1953

1959

1969

1981

A collection of Karo ads from 1904 to 1981.

The KARO COOK BOOK

RECIPE COLLECTOR'S EDITION

All the recipes in this cookbook were developed and tested by home economists in the Best Foods kitchens.

Prepared by Best Foods, a Unit of CPC North America
Englewood Cliffs, New Jersey 07632

Photography by Lynn St. John

Production and printing by Davis-Delaney-Arrow
A TCI Company, New York City

Table of Contents

Who was KARO?

Who was the mystery woman Karo was named for?

Karo Corn Syrup.
Invented by a man.
Named for a woman.

Some say her name was Caroline.

Some say she was his wife.

Some say she wasn't.

It's still a bit mysterious. And more than a little romantic. But women have loved creating with Karo, since Karo was created in 1902. And it's been a loving touch in great American cooking since the turn of the century.

It was a romantic time for America. It was the age of linen and lace, and sweet innocence. And Karo became part of the American language. In parts of the country to this day, Pecan Pie is known as Karo Pie. Because no other ingredient can produce that characteristic flavor and texture.

$\mathcal{B}$ut if you thought Karo corn syrup was only for pecan pie and candy making—look again...

Karo is a valued companion to other good native foods, playing a warm and graceful role in favorite regional dishes. Karo's versatility can be seen in fresh salads and vegetables as well as hearty main meals. Karo glazes and marinades provide a loving touch and indeed can make even leftovers special. And desserts made with Karo climax a fine meal, beverages add sparkle to a party and Karo gifts of candies and cookies bring joy to the recipient. Karo corn syrup has given pleasure to generations of American cooks and lovers of good eating.

Today the heritage of good American cooking is being richly revived. Once again there is a pride in doing things well. Karo belongs to this tradition. And so it is with great pleasure that the makers of Karo corn syrup present this new album of recipes. Long-time Karo fans will find it contains many of their favorites as well as an exciting array of new recipes. But for the newcomer to Karo corn syrup, there are also answers to basic questions about Karo's use, tips to help personalize cooking and quick and simple recipe ideas to try.

Questions and Answers About Corn Syrup

What is corn syrup?

Corn syrup is a thick concentrated solution of dextrose and other sugars derived from corn starch. It is mildly sweet and improves and enhances the flavor and texture of many foods.

What is the difference between light and dark corn syrup?

Karo light corn syrup is a mixture of corn syrup and high fructose corn syrup (to provide sweetness) and is flavored with salt and pure vanilla.

Karo dark corn syrup is a mixture of corn syrup and a small amount of refiner's syrup (a cane sugar product with a molasses-like flavor). Caramel flavor, sodium benzoate, salt and caramel color are added.

Can Karo light corn syrup and Karo dark corn syrup be used interchangeably?

Yes. Taste preferences and recipe directions are the best guides in helping you choose. Light corn syrup is usually used where extra flavoring or color is not desirable. Dark corn syrup provides a rich brown color and a distinctive moderately sweet flavor.

Can corn syrup be substituted for granulated sugar in recipes?

Although corn syrup and sugars are both sweeteners, it is not possible to use them interchangeably in all recipes. Since corn syrup is a liquid, it cannot replace sugar on an equal basis and other ingredients in the recipe must be adjusted, particularly in baked goods. For best results, follow recipes which have been developed especially for corn syrup.

How should corn syrup be stored?
Unopened corn syrup may be stored at room temperatures. Refrigeration, after opening, will prolong the shelf life of the syrup.

Can Karo be used as a pour-on syrup?
Yes, many people pour it straight from the bottle onto waffles, pancakes, fruit, ice cream and cereals.

What type of main dishes call for Karo?
Karo is an ideal ingredient in sweet and sour combinations. Although well known as a glaze for ham, it works well as a glaze for other meats. It also adds flavor to many regional dishes such as chili con carne and baked beans.

How does Karo fit into vegetable cookery?
Anytime a touch of sweetness is called for, Karo can help. It glazes sweet potatoes and squash, sweetens baked bean dishes and blends flavors in vegetable marinades.

What role does Karo play in salad making?
Karo adds smoothness to salad dressings and helps blend flavors of salad ingredients.

Why is Karo used in making ice cream and sherbets?
Karo prevents the formation of large ice crystals, making a smoother, creamier product.

What is the function of Karo in candy making?
Karo controls sugar crystal formation in candies.

How is Karo used in home canned fruits, jams and preserves?
While up to 25% of the sugar can be replaced with corn syrup to improve appearance, flavor and consistency, it is best to follow recipes developed especially with Karo.

MAIN DISHES, NICE AND EASY

Whether for lunch or for dinner, for family or honored guests, the main course is the centerpiece of a meal. It deserves special thought and attention, but need not take undue labor in the kitchen. Instead, begin with quality ingredients and add creativity and originality. Karo can help recreate family favorites and inspire new traditions.

SURF AND TURF KABOBS

1/4 cup corn oil	1/4 teaspoon pepper
1/4 cup soy sauce	1/2 pound top round steak, cut in 16 cubes
1/4 cup Karo dark corn syrup	16 shrimp, shelled, deveined
1/4 cup lemon juice	16 large mushroom caps
2 tablespoons prepared mustard	1 medium zucchini, cut in 16 (1-inch) pieces
2 cloves garlic, minced	8 cherry tomatoes
1/2 teaspoon ground ginger	

In bowl stir together corn oil, soy sauce, corn syrup, lemon juice, mustard, garlic, ginger and pepper. In large shallow dish place beef, shrimp and mushrooms. Pour marinade over beef mixture. Cover; chill several hours or overnight. Remove from marinade. On each of 8 skewers, alternately thread zucchini, beef, shrimp and mushrooms. Grill 6 inches from heat, turning and basting frequently, 10 minutes or until desired doneness. During last 2 minutes of cooking, thread cherry tomatoes on each skewer. Makes 4 servings.

Top: *Apricot Glaze for Ham* p. 37.
Bottom: *Spicy Beef and Vegetables* p. 12.

SPICY BEEF AND VEGETABLES

4 tablespoons corn
  starch
1 can (10 1/2 oz)
  condensed beef
  broth
1/3 cup Karo dark corn
  syrup
1/3 cup soy sauce
1/2 teaspoon crushed
  dried red pepper
1 pound flank steak
6 tablespoons corn oil
1 cup carrot strips

2 medium onions, cut
  in thin wedges
1/2 pound mushrooms,
  sliced
1 package (6 oz) frozen
  snow peas, thawed,
  drained
1 can (8 oz) water chest-
  nuts, drained, sliced
2 cloves garlic, minced
  Cooked rice

In bowl mix corn starch and beef broth until smooth. Stir in corn syrup, soy sauce and red pepper. Cut steak in half lengthwise; slice each half, across the grain, into 1/8-inch thick slices. In wok or large skillet heat 4 tablespoons of the corn oil over medium-high heat. Add carrots and onion; stir fry 2 minutes. Add mushrooms, snow peas and water chestnuts. Stir fry 2 minutes or until tender-crisp. With slotted spoon remove vegetables to bowl. Heat remaining 2 tablespoons corn oil. Add steak and garlic. Stir fry 3 minutes or until tender. Stir corn starch mixture; add to beef mixture. Add vegetables. Stirring constantly, bring to boil over medium heat and boil 1 minute. Serve over rice. Makes 4 to 6 servings.

KOREAN STYLE FLANK STEAK

1/4 cup sesame seeds
1/4 cup corn oil
1/4 cup soy sauce
1/4 cup Karo dark corn
  syrup
1 small onion, sliced

1 clove garlic, minced
1/4 teaspoon pepper
1/4 teaspoon ground
  ginger
1 1/2 pounds flank
  steak, scored

In shallow dish stir together sesame seeds, corn oil, soy sauce, corn syrup, onion, garlic, pepper and ginger. Add steak, turning to coat. Chill, turning once, several hours or overnight. Grill 6 inches from heat, turning once, about 8 minutes or until desired doneness. Slice diagonally across grain. Makes about 6 servings.

Korean Style Chicken: Follow recipe for Korean Style Flank Steak. Substitute 1 broiler-fryer chicken, cut in parts, for flank steak. Bake in 375°F oven, basting occasionally, 45 minutes or until tender. Or grill over low heat, turning and basting frequently, about 50 minutes. Makes 4 servings.

Korean Style Fish: Follow recipe for Korean Style Flank Steak. Substitute 1 1/2 pounds fish fillets for flank steak. Broil 4 inches from heat, turning once, 4 to 5 minutes or until fish flakes easily. Or grill over low heat 3 to 4 minutes on each side. Makes 6 servings.

AUTUMN BEEF STEW

1/4 cup corn oil	Dash crushed dried
2 pounds stew beef, cut	red pepper
in 1 1/2-inch cubes	2 sweet potatoes,
1 1/2 cups chopped onion	peeled, sliced,
1 1/2 cups dry red wine	1/2-inch thick
1/2 cup Karo dark corn	1 teaspoon grated
syrup	lemon rind
1 1/2 teaspoons salt	1 large apple, cut in
1/2 teaspoon dried thyme	eighths
leaves	2 tablespoons corn
1/2 teaspoon dried	starch
marjoram leaves	1/4 cup water
1/4 teaspoon ground	
cinnamon	

In 5-quart dutch oven heat corn oil over medium-high heat. Add beef, 1/2 at a time, and brown on all sides. Remove beef. Add onion; sauté 5 minutes. Reduce heat. Stir in wine, corn syrup, salt, thyme, marjoram, cinnamon and red pepper. Add beef. Bring to boil. Reduce heat; cover and simmer 30 minutes. Add potatoes and lemon rind. Cover and simmer, stirring occasionally, 15 minutes. Add apple and simmer 15 minutes longer. Mix corn starch and water until smooth. Stir into beef mixture. Stirring constantly, bring to boil over medium heat and boil 1 minute. Makes 8 servings.

BEEF TERIYAKI

1/4 cup Karo dark corn syrup	1/2 teaspoon ground ginger
1/4 cup soy sauce	1 clove garlic, minced
2 tablespoons dry white wine	1 1/4 pounds flank steak, scored

In shallow dish stir together corn syrup, soy sauce, wine, ginger and garlic. Add steak, turning to coat. Cover; chill, turning occasionally, several hours or overnight. Broil 6 inches from heat, turning and basting once, about 8 minutes or until desired doneness. Slice diagonally across grain. Makes about 4 servings.

Chicken Teriyaki: Follow recipe for Beef Teriyaki. Substitute 2 whole chicken breasts, boned, skinned, cut in 1 1/2-inch cubes, for flank steak. Chill, turning occasionally, several hours or overnight. Thread chicken onto small skewers. Broil 6 inches from heat, turning and basting frequently, about 5 minutes or until chicken is tender and browned. Makes 4 servings.

Fish Teriyaki: Follow recipe for Beef Teriyaki. Substitute 2 (1-inch) salmon, snapper or halibut steaks for flank steak. Broil 6 inches from heat, turning and basting once, about 8 minutes or until fish flakes easily. Makes 2 to 3 servings.

GINGER FLAVORED LONDON BROIL

1/2 cup Karo dark corn syrup	2 cloves garlic, sliced
1/4 cup soy sauce	1 (3 lb) boneless beef shoulder roast, 2-inches thick
2 tablespoons cider vinegar	
2 teaspoons ground ginger	

In large shallow dish stir together corn syrup, soy sauce, vinegar, ginger and garlic. Add steak, turning to coat. Cover; chill, turning at least once, overnight. Grill 6 inches from heat, turning and basting frequently, 25 to 30 minutes or until desired doneness. Slice diagonally across grain. Makes 6 to 8 servings.

HAWAIIAN FRANKS

1 tablespoon corn oil	2 tablespoons white vinegar
1 pound frankfurters, cut in 1-inch pieces	1 teaspoon ground ginger
1 medium green pepper, coarsely chopped	1/2 teaspoon dry·mustard
1 can (13 1/2 oz) pineapple chunks in heavy syrup	2 tablespoons corn starch
1/2 cup Karo dark corn syrup	1/4 cup water
3 tablespoons soy sauce	1 can (8 oz) water chestnuts, drained, sliced

In skillet heat corn oil over medium heat. Add frankfurters; cook 3 minutes or until lightly browned. Add pepper. Stirring constantly, cook about 2 minutes or until tender. Drain pineapple; reserve syrup. In small bowl stir together pineapple syrup, corn syrup, soy sauce, vinegar, ginger and mustard. Add to skillet; bring to boil. Mix corn starch and water. Stir into mixture in skillet. Stirring constantly, bring to boil over medium heat and boil 1 minute. Add pineapple chunks and water chestnuts. Cook until heated. Makes 4 servings.

FRANKS WITH SAUERKRAUT

2 tablespoons margarine	1 cup shredded carrots
1 pound frankfurters, cut in half crosswise	1/2 cup tomato juice
1 can (16 oz) sauerkraut	1/3 cup Karo dark corn syrup
1 cup chopped green apple	2 teaspoons caraway seeds

In large skillet melt margarine over medium heat. Add frankfurters; cook 2 to 3 minutes or until browned. Add sauerkraut, apple, carrot, tomato juice, corn syrup and caraway seeds. Bring to boil over medium heat. Reduce heat and simmer 20 minutes or until heated. Makes 4 servings.

MEXICAN FRANKFURTERS

1/2 cup catchup	1 cup coarsely chopped
1/4 cup Karo dark corn	onion
syrup	1 can (15 oz) pinto or
1/4 cup corn oil	kidney beans,
2 tablespoons prepared	drained, rinsed
spicy brown	1 can (4 oz) chopped
mustard	green chilies,
2 tablespoons chili	drained
powder	8 frankfurters, scored
2 tablespoons corn oil	8 frankfurter rolls, split

In small bowl stir together catchup, corn syrup, 1/4 cup corn oil, mustard and chili powder. In skillet heat 2 tablespoons corn oil over medium heat. Add onion; sauté 2 minutes. Stir in beans, chilies and 1 cup catchup mixture. Place frankfurters on rack in broiler pan. Brush with remaining catchup mixture. Broil 6 inches from heat, turning and basting with catchup mixture, 5 to 7 minutes or until evenly browned and heated through. Spoon 1/4 cup bean mixture into each frankfurter roll; top with frankfurter. Makes 8 servings.

SWEDISH STYLE STUFFED CABBAGE

2 quarts water	1/4 cup Karo light or dark
1 tablespoon salt	corn syrup
1 (3 lb) cabbage	1 1/2 teaspoons salt
1/2 cup margarine	1/4 teaspoon white pepper
1/2 pound chopped	1/4 teaspoon ground
mushrooms	allspice
1 cup chopped onion	3/4 cup water
1 clove garlic, minced	1/3 cup corn starch
1 pound ground beef	1/2 cup water
1 pound ground pork	
2 hard-cooked eggs,	
chopped	

In large saucepot bring 2 quarts water and salt to boil over medium-high heat. Add cabbage. Boil 5 to 10 minutes. Remove cabbage. Reserve 2 cups cabbage liquid. Carefully remove 12 leaves from cabbage. Drain. In 5-quart dutch oven melt 1/4 cup of the margarine over medium heat. Add mushrooms, onion and garlic. Sauté 5 minutes. Remove from heat. In large bowl stir together mushroom mixture, beef, pork, eggs, 2 tablespoons of the corn syrup, salt, pepper and allspice until well mixed. Gradually add 3/4 cup water. (Mixture should be quite moist.) Place about 1/2 cup meat mixture on each cabbage leaf. Fold sides of cabbage leaves over meat; roll up. In dutch oven heat remaining margarine and remaining corn syrup over medium heat until margarine is melted. Add cabbage rolls, 4 at a time, and cook until glazed on all sides. Return to dutch oven. Add reserved cabbage liquid. Cook over low heat 40 minutes. Remove cabbage rolls. Mix corn starch and 1/2 cup water until smooth. Add to liquid. Stirring constantly, bring to boil over medium heat and boil 1 minute. Spoon over cabbage rolls. Makes 6 servings.

DEVILED BURGERS

1	pound ground beef	1/3	cup bottled steak sauce
1	cup sliced onion, separated into rings	1	tablespoon prepared spicy brown mustard
1/2	cup Karo dark corn syrup		

Shape beef into 4 oval patties, 1/2-inch thick. Heat skillet over medium-high heat. Add patties; cook, turning once, 10 minutes or until desired doneness. Remove to platter; keep warm. Pour off all but 2 tablespoons drippings. Add onion; sauté 3 minutes. Stir in corn syrup, steak sauce and mustard. Bring to boil. Spoon over burgers. Makes 4 servings.

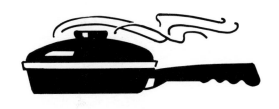

WESTERN STYLE CASSEROLE

1 pound ground beef
1/4 cup chopped onion
1 can (16 oz) whole
   kernel corn, drained
1 can (16 oz) red kidney
   beans, drained
1 can (10 3/4 oz) con-
   densed tomato soup
1 cup shredded Cheddar
   cheese

1/4 cup Karo dark corn
   syrup
1/4 cup milk
1 tablespoon chili
   powder
1 cup buttermilk baking
   mix
1/3 cup milk

In large skillet cook beef and onion over medium heat 5 minutes or until browned. Stir in corn, beans, soup, cheese, corn syrup, 1/4 cup milk and chili powder. Spoon into 2-quart casserole. Bake in 450°F oven 20 to 25 minutes or until bubbly. In medium bowl with fork beat buttermilk baking mix and 1/3 cup milk until blended (mixture will be thick). Drop by spoonfuls on top of beef mixture. Bake in 400°F oven 25 minutes or until biscuits are golden. Makes 8 servings.

CHILI CON CARNE

1 tablespoon corn oil
1 cup sliced onion
1 clove garlic, minced
1 pound lean chuck, cut
   in 1/4-inch cubes
1/2 cup Karo dark corn
   syrup
3 tablespoons chili
   powder
1 teaspoon ground
   cumin

2 cans (16 oz each)
   whole tomatoes
2 cans (15 oz each) red
   kidney beans
1 can (15 oz) pinto
   beans or light
   kidney beans
1 can (4 oz) whole green
   chilies, drained

In 5-quart dutch oven heat corn oil over medium-high heat. Add onion and garlic; sauté 5 minutes. Remove from pan. Add beef, 1/3 at a time, and brown on all sides. Return onion and garlic to pan. Add corn syrup, chili powder and cumin. Stirring frequently, bring to boil. Stir in tomatoes, beans and chilies. Reduce heat. Simmer 1 to 2 hours or until thickened and meat is tender. Makes 12 servings.

FRENCH BREAD PIZZA STYLE

1 pound ground beef
1/2 cup chopped onion
1/4 cup Karo light or dark
   corn syrup
1 can (6 oz) tomato paste
1/4 cup grated Parmesan
   cheese
1/4 cup sliced ripe olives

1 teaspoon dried
   oregano leaves
1/2 teaspoon salt
1/4 teaspoon pepper
1 loaf French bread, split
   in half lengthwise
1 cup shredded Cheddar
   cheese

In large skillet brown beef and onion over medium heat. Add corn syrup, tomato paste, Parmesan cheese, olives, oregano, salt and pepper. Cook 10 minutes longer. Spoon beef mixture on cut sides of bread. Sprinkle with Cheddar cheese. Bake in 400°F oven 5 minutes or until cheese is melted. Makes 4 servings.

TOKYO MEATBALLS

1 pound ground beef
1/2 cup soft bread crumbs
1/2 cup finely chopped
   celery
2 tablespoons corn oil
1/2 cup chopped onion
1 clove garlic, minced
1 1/2 cups sliced
   mushrooms

1/2 cup Karo light corn
   syrup
1/3 cup dry white wine
2 tablespoons soy sauce
1/4 teaspoon ground
   ginger
2 teaspoons corn starch
2 tablespoons water

In bowl mix together beef, bread crumbs and celery. Shape into 1-inch balls. In large skillet heat corn oil over medium-high heat. Add meatballs and brown on all sides. Remove to platter; keep warm. Pour off all but 2 tablespoons drippings. Add onion and garlic. Sauté 3 minutes. Add mushrooms; cook 1 minute or until tender. Stir in corn syrup, wine, soy sauce and ginger. Bring to boil. Mix corn starch and water. Stir into soy sauce mixture. Stirring constantly, bring to boil over medium heat and boil 1 minute. Pour sauce over meatballs. Makes 4 to 5 servings.

APPLE BEEF LOAF

1 can (8 oz) tomato sauce	1/2 cup fine dry bread crumbs
1/4 cup Karo light corn syrup	1/2 cup finely chopped onion
2 tablespoons prepared mustard	1 teaspoon salt
2 eggs, slightly beaten	1/2 teaspoon ground nutmeg
1 cup finely chopped peeled apple	1/8 teaspoon pepper
	1 1/2 pounds ground beef

In small bowl stir together tomato sauce, corn syrup and mustard. In large bowl mix 3/4 cup tomato mixture, egg, apple, bread crumbs, onion, salt, nutmeg and pepper. Add beef; toss to blend. In 11 x 7 x 2-inch baking dish form beef mixture into loaf. Bake in 350°F oven 30 minutes. Cover with remaining tomato sauce mixture. Bake 30 minutes longer. Makes 6 to 8 servings.

Tip: Apple Beef Loaf is an ideal choice for a main dish at a special family meal. To garnish, arrange apple slices attractively across the top.

MEXICALI BEEF PIE

1 pound ground beef	1 cup shredded Cheddar cheese
1/2 cup chopped onion	1/4 cup raisins
1/4 cup chopped green pepper	1/4 cup Karo dark corn syrup
1 clove garlic, minced	1 tablespoon chili powder
2 tablespoons corn starch	1/2 teaspoon salt
1 can (8 3/4 oz) red kidney beans, drained	1 unbaked (9-inch) pastry shell
1 cup coarsely chopped tomatoes	

In large skillet cook beef, onion, green pepper and garlic over medium heat about 10 minutes or until meat is browned. Drain off fat. Add corn starch; toss to coat meat. Add beans, tomatoes, 1/2 cup of the cheese, raisins, corn syrup, chili powder and salt. Stirring constantly, cook over medium heat 2 minutes or until color brightens and mixture holds together. Spoon into pastry shell; sprinkle with remaining cheese. Bake in 400°F oven 20 minutes or until heated. Makes 6 to 8 servings.

STUFFED TOMATOES

6	large tomatoes	1	teaspoon salt
1/2	pound ground beef	1/4	teaspoon pepper
1/2	cup chopped onion	1	cup herb-seasoned
1/2	cup chopped green		stuffing mix
	pepper	1/4	cup grated Parmesan
1/4	cup Karo dark corn		cheese
	syrup	3	ounces mozzarella
1	tablespoon Worcester-		cheese, shredded
	shire sauce		(3/4 cup)
1	teaspoon dried basil		
	leaves		

Cut tops off tomatoes; scoop out pulp. Chop tops and pulp; drain. In large skillet brown beef, onion and pepper over medium heat about 5 minutes. Add chopped tomatoes, corn syrup, Worcestershire sauce, basil, salt and pepper. Stirring frequently, cook 10 minutes or until thick and bubbly. Remove from heat. Add stuffing mix and Parmesan cheese. Spoon into tomato shells. Place tomatoes in 11 x 7 x 2-inch baking dish. Top each tomato with 2 tablespoons mozzarella. Bake in 350°F oven 25 to 30 minutes or until heated. Makes 6 servings.

ORANGE GLAZED PORK CHOPS

2 tablespoons corn oil	1/4 teaspoon ground ginger
6 loin pork chops, 3/4-inch thick	1/8 teaspoon ground cloves
1 1/2 cups orange juice	1/8 teaspoon pepper
3/4 cup Karo light corn syrup	1 package (11 oz) mixed dried fruit
3 tablespoons lemon juice	2 tablespoons corn starch
1 teaspoon salt	2 tablespoons water
1/4 teaspoon ground cinnamon	

In large skillet heat corn oil over medium heat; add chops and brown on both sides. Drain off fat. In small bowl stir together orange juice, corn syrup, lemon juice, salt, cinnamon, ginger, cloves and pepper. Pour over chops. Top with dried fruit. Cover. Cook over low heat about 45 minutes or until tender. Arrange chops and fruit on serving platter. Mix corn starch and water; stir into mixture in skillet. Stirring constantly, bring to boil over medium heat and boil 1 minute. Serve with chops and fruit. Makes 6 servings.

LIME FLAVORED PORK CHOPS

1/3 cup Karo dark corn syrup	1 tablespoon soy sauce
1/2 teaspoon grated lime rind	1/4 teaspoon ground cloves
1/3 cup lime juice	6 loin pork chops, 1-inch thick

In small bowl stir together corn syrup, lime rind, lime juice, soy sauce and cloves. Grill chops 6 inches from heat, turning once, 30 minutes. Baste with lime mixture. Grill 30 minutes longer, turning and basting frequently, or until pork is tender and glazed. Makes 6 servings.

Tip: Although Lime Flavored Pork Chops are delicious grilled outdoors, if the weather suddenly turns bad, they can also be successfully broiled indoors.

WESTERN PORK CHOPS

2 tablespoons
    margarine
4 loin pork chops (about
    1 1/2 lb)
1 cup chopped green
    pepper

1 cup chopped onion
1 can (8 oz) tomato
    sauce
1/2 cup Karo light or dark
    corn syrup
3/4 teaspoon chili powder

In skillet melt margarine over medium heat. Add chops and brown on both sides. Remove chops. Add pepper and onion; sauté 5 minutes. Stir in tomato sauce, corn syrup and chili powder. Return chops to skillet. Bring to boil; reduce heat and simmer about 30 minutes or until tender. If desired, serve over noodles. Makes 4 servings.

TANGY PORK CHOPS

1/4 cup unsifted flour
1 teaspoon salt
1/4 teaspoon pepper
4 loin pork chops,
    3/4-inch thick
2 tablespoons margarine
1 can (20 oz) pineapple
    chunks in own juice

3/4 cup Karo light corn
    syrup
1/3 cup lemon juice
3 tablespoons catchup
2 tablespoons soy sauce
1 medium green pepper,
    cut in thin strips
Cooked rice or noodles

In shallow dish or on sheet of waxed paper combine flour, salt and pepper. Coat chops with flour mixture; with meat mallet pound chops on both sides. In large skillet melt margarine over medium heat. Add chops and cook, turning once, about 20 minutes or until browned and tender. Remove chops. Drain off fat. Keep warm. In same skillet stir together undrained pineapple, corn syrup, lemon juice, catchup and soy sauce. Stirring occasionally, boil about 25 minutes or until reduced by half. Add green pepper; cook 1 minute. Serve pork and sauce over rice. Makes 4 servings.

23

SIERRA RANCH RIBS

4 pounds country-style spareribs, trimmed, cut in serving pieces
Water
1 can (8 oz) tomato sauce
1 cup chopped onion
1/2 cup Karo dark corn syrup
1/4 cup cider vinegar
2 tablespoons Worcestershire sauce
1 teaspoon salt
1 teaspoon dry mustard
1/2 teaspoon chili powder

In 5-quart saucepot place spareribs; add water to depth of 1-inch; cover. Bring to boil over high heat; reduce heat and boil gently 1 hour or until tender. In 1-quart saucepan stir together tomato sauce, onion, corn syrup, vinegar, Worcestershire sauce, salt, mustard and chili powder. Bring to boil; reduce heat and simmer 10 minutes. Drain ribs well. Brush generously with sauce. Grill ribs 6 inches from heat, turning and basting frequently, about 15 minutes or until browned. Or broil 4 inches from heat, turning once and basting occasionally, about 20 minutes. Heat remaining sauce and serve with ribs. Makes 6 to 8 servings.

ZESTY RIBS

4 pounds spareribs, cut in 2-inch riblets
1 tablespoon margarine
1/2 cup chopped onion
1/4 cup chopped prunes
1/4 cup lemon juice
1/4 cup Karo light corn syrup
2 tablespoons soy sauce
2 tablespoons catchup
1 teaspoon Worcestershire sauce
1/2 teaspoon ground ginger
2 drops hot pepper sauce

Place ribs on rack in shallow roasting pan. Bake in 400°F oven, turning once, 40 minutes or until tender. In small skillet melt margarine over medium heat. Add onion; sauté 3 minutes. Place onion, prunes, lemon juice, corn syrup, soy sauce, catchup, Worcestershire sauce, ginger and hot pepper sauce into blender container; cover. Blend on high speed 30 seconds or until smooth. Brush ribs with sauce. Bake 20 minutes longer, turning and basting once, or until sauce is heated. Makes about 24.

GINGER PLUM SPARERIBS

1 jar (10 oz) damson plum or apple jelly	2 cloves garlic, minced
1/3 cup Karo dark corn syrup	2 teaspoons ground ginger
1/3 cup soy sauce	2 pounds country-style spareribs, trimmed, cut in serving pieces
1/4 cup chopped green onion	

In small saucepan mix jelly, corn syrup, soy sauce, onion, garlic and ginger. Stirring constantly, cook over medium heat until jelly is melted. Pour into 11 x 7 x 2-inch baking dish. Add ribs. Cover; chill, turning once, several hours or overnight. Remove from marinade and place on rack in shallow baking pan. Bake in 350°F oven, turning as needed and basting with marinade, about 1 hour or until tender. Makes 4 servings.

Ginger Plum Chicken Wings: Follow recipe for Ginger Plum Spareribs. Substitute 2 1/2 pounds chicken wings, separated at the joints (tips discarded). Bake 45 minutes, basting with marinade during last 1/2 hour.

FRUITED LOIN OF PORK

1 cup (about) dried apricots	1/2 cup Karo dark corn syrup
1/2 cup dry sherry	1 tablespoon grated orange rind
1 (3 to 5 lb) center cut pork loin roast, backbone cracked	1/4 cup orange juice
	1/2 teaspoon soy sauce

In small saucepan stir together apricots and sherry. Cover and cook over medium heat, stirring occasionally, until liquid is absorbed. Cut deep slits between each pork chop. Insert 3 or 4 apricots in each slit. Place pork on rack in roasting pan. Roast in 325°F oven 2 to 3 hours or until meat thermometer registers 170°F. Meanwhile, in small saucepan stir together corn syrup, orange rind, juice and soy sauce. Bring to boil; reduce heat and simmer 3 minutes. Brush pork frequently with glaze during last 30 minutes of roasting time. Makes 6 to 10 servings.

ROAST PORK WITH RUBY GLAZE

1 (4 to 6 lb) boneless
   pork loin roast
   (double loin, rolled,
   tied)
2 cups cranberries

1 cup Karo light corn
   syrup
1 cup sugar
1/4 teaspoon ground
   cinnamon

Line shallow roasting pan with foil; place roast, fat side up, on rack in pan. Roast in 325°F oven 2 1/2 to 3 hours or until meat thermometer registers 170°F. Meanwhile, in 2-quart saucepan bring cranberries, corn syrup, sugar and cinnamon to boil over medium heat. Stirring frequently, boil 2 minutes. Remove from heat; let stand at room temperature. Drain 1/2 cup liquid from cranberry glaze. Brush on pork several times during last 40 minutes of roasting. Serve remaining glaze as sauce for roast. Makes 10 to 12 servings.

QUICK SWEET AND SOUR PORK

2 tablespoons corn oil
1 pound boneless pork,
   cut in 1-inch cubes
1 can (20 oz) pineapple
   chunks in own juice
1/2 cup Karo light or dark
   corn syrup
1/4 cup cider vinegar
2 tablespoons catchup

2 tablespoons soy sauce
1 clove garlic, minced
1 small green pepper,
   cut in 1-inch squares
2 tablespoons corn
   starch
2 tablespoons water
Cooked rice

In large skillet heat corn oil over medium-high heat; add pork and brown on all sides. Add undrained pineapple, corn syrup, vinegar, catchup, soy sauce and garlic. Bring to boil; reduce heat and simmer, stirring occasionally, 10 minutes or until pork is tender. Add pepper. Mix corn starch and water; stir into pork mixture. Stirring constantly, bring to boil over medium heat and boil 1 minute. Serve over rice. Makes 4 servings.

Top to bottom: *Easy Sesame Chicken* p. 33,
Marinated Lamb Kabobs p. 29, *Apple Beef Loaf* p. 20.

OLD FASHIONED HAM LOAF

1/2 cup Karo dark corn syrup	1/2 cup fine dry bread crumbs
1/4 cup white vinegar	1/4 teaspoon pepper
2 tablespoons prepared mustard	1 1/2 pounds ground cooked ham (4 1/2 cups)
1 tablespoon prepared horseradish	1/2 pound ground pork
1 egg, beaten	1 orange, peeled, thinly sliced
1/2 cup water	

In small bowl stir together corn syrup, vinegar, mustard and horseradish. In large bowl mix egg, water, bread crumbs and pepper. Add ham, pork and 1/2 of the corn syrup mixture. Toss until well blended. Press ham mixture into 9 x 5 x 3-inch loaf pan. Turn into 11 x 7 x 2-inch baking dish. Pour remaining corn syrup mixture over loaf. Bake in 350°F oven, basting occasionally, 1 hour. Top with orange slices, baste, and bake 15 minutes longer. Makes 6 to 8 servings.

GLAZED HAM

3/4 cup Karo dark corn syrup	1 (12 to 15 lb) fully cooked ham with bone in
1/2 cup firmly packed brown sugar	

In bowl mix corn syrup and brown sugar. Line large roasting pan with foil. Score ham about 1/2-inch deep. Place ham on rack in prepared pan. Roast in 325°F oven 3 1/2 to 4 hours or until meat thermometer registers 140°F. About 30 minutes before ham is done, brush frequently with corn syrup mixture. Serve warm or cold. Makes about 30 servings.

Tip: When time is short, a very satisfactory glaze can be made by simply pouring light or dark Karo onto the ham for the last half hour of baking.

MARINATED LAMB KABOBS

1/2 cup Karo dark corn
    syrup
1/2 cup dry red wine
1/4 cup corn oil
  2 cloves garlic, minced
1 1/2 teaspoons dried
    oregano leaves
  1 teaspoon salt
1/4 teaspoon pepper

1 pound boneless lamb,
    cut in 1 1/2-inch
    cubes
2 medium onions, cut
    in wedges
1 green pepper, cut in
    1-inch squares
6 cherry tomatoes

In large shallow dish stir together corn syrup, wine, corn oil, garlic, oregano, salt and pepper. Add lamb; toss to coat. Cover; chill, turning occasionally, several hours or overnight. Thread lamb, onion and green pepper alternately on 6 (6-inch) skewers. Broil 6 inches from heat, turning and basting occasionally, 15 minutes or until desired doneness. During last 2 minutes add 1 cherry tomato to each skewer. Makes 6 servings.

SWEET AND SOUR LAMB CHOPS

4 shoulder lamb chops,
    1-inch thick
1/4 cup Karo light corn
    syrup
  2 tablespoons lemon
    juice
  1 teaspoon dried mint
    leaves
  1 teaspoon salt

1/2 teaspoon ground
    ginger
1/8 teaspoon pepper
  1 orange, peeled, cut in
    4 thick slices
  1 tablespoon corn
    starch
  1 cup water

In 5-quart dutch oven cook chops over medium-high heat, turning once, 10 minutes or until well browned. In small bowl mix corn syrup, lemon juice, mint, salt, ginger and pepper. Pour over chops. Top each chop with orange slice. Reduce heat. Cover and simmer 30 minutes or until chops are tender. Remove chops and place on serving platter. Mix corn starch and water until smooth. Stir into liquid in skillet. Stirring constantly, bring to boil over medium heat and boil 1 minute. Makes 4 servings.

LAMB STUFFED SQUASH

3 medium acorn
squash, halved,
seeded
1 1/2 cups water
2 tablespoons
margarine, melted
2 tablespoons Karo dark
corn syrup
1/2 pound ground lamb
1/2 cup chopped onion
1 cup cooked rice
1/3 cup raisins

1/4 cup chopped parsley
3 tablespoons Karo dark
corn syrup
1 tablespoon white
vinegar
1 teaspoon salt
1/2 teaspoon ground
cinnamon
1/4 teaspoon pepper
1/4 teaspoon ground
nutmeg

Place squash cut-side down in 13 x 9 x 2-inch baking dish.
Add water. Bake in 400°F oven 30 minutes or until firm.
Drain water. Turn squash cut-side up. In small bowl stir
margarine and 2 tablespoons corn syrup. Brush squash with
corn syrup mixture. Bake in 350°F oven 15 minutes or until
tender. In skillet brown lamb and onion over medium heat
about 5 minutes or until well browned. Add rice, raisins,
parsley, 3 tablespoons corn syrup, vinegar, salt, cinnamon,
pepper and nutmeg. Reduce heat; simmer 5 minutes. Spoon
1/2 cup lamb mixture into each squash half. Bake in 350°F
oven 5 minutes or until heated. Makes 6 servings.

CHICKEN WITH CRANBERRIES

1 (3 to 4 lb) roasting
chicken
1 cup cranberries
1 cup Karo light corn
syrup

1/2 cup dry white wine
2 tablespoons corn oil

Place chicken on rack in small shallow roasting pan. Bake in
375°F oven 1 hour. Meanwhile, in blender container place
cranberries, corn syrup, wine and corn oil; cover. Blend at
high speed 1 minute or until smooth. Basting chicken frequently with glaze, bake 30 minutes longer or until meat
thermometer registers 185°F. In small saucepan heat remaining glaze and serve with chicken. Makes 4 servings.

LEMON GLAZED CHICKEN

2 tablespoons margarine	1/2 cup chicken broth
1 broiler-fryer chicken, cut in parts	1/4 cup lemon juice
1/2 cup Karo light or dark corn syrup	1/4 teaspoon salt

In large skillet melt margarine over medium heat. Add chicken and cook about 35 minutes or until browned on all sides and tender. Remove chicken; drain off fat. Keep warm. In same skillet stir together corn syrup, chicken broth, lemon juice and salt. Stirring frequently, boil 10 minutes or until slightly thickened. Spoon over chicken. Makes 4 servings.

SWEET AND SOUR CHICKEN

1/4 cup margarine	3 tablespoons catchup
1 broiler-fryer chicken, cut in parts	2 tablespoons soy sauce
1 can (15 1/4 oz) pineapple chunks in own juice	2 tablespoons corn starch
3/4 cup Karo light corn syrup	2 tablespoons water
3 tablespoons cider vinegar	1 medium green pepper, cut in strips
	Cooked rice or noodles

In large skillet melt margarine over medium heat. Add chicken and cook about 35 minutes or until browned on all sides and tender. Remove chicken; drain off fat. Keep warm. In same skillet stir together undrained pineapple, corn syrup, vinegar, catchup and soy sauce. Stirring frequently, boil rapidly 5 minutes. Mix corn starch and water until smooth; stir into liquid in skillet. Add pepper. Stirring constantly, bring to boil over medium heat and boil 1 minute. Arrange chicken on rice; spoon sauce over chicken. Makes 4 servings.

31

ISLAND CHICKEN DELIGHT

1/4 cup margarine
1 broiler-fryer chicken, cut in parts
1 can (14 oz) pineapple chunks in own juice
1/2 cup Karo light or dark corn syrup
1 medium orange, sliced
1 medium lemon, sliced

In large skillet melt margarine over medium heat. Add chicken and cook about 35 minutes or until browned on all sides and tender. Remove chicken; drain off fat. In same skillet stir together undrained pineapple and corn syrup; top with orange and lemon slices. Bring to boil; boil 2 minutes. Remove orange and lemon slices; arrange with chicken on platter. Keep warm. Stirring frequently, boil pineapple mixture about 15 minutes or until slightly thick and syrupy; spoon over chicken. Makes 4 servings.

PINEAPPLE BARBECUED CHICKEN

1 can (8 oz) crushed pineapple in own juice
1/2 cup Karo dark corn syrup
2 tablespoons lemon juice
2 tablespoons soy sauce
1/2 teaspoon salt
1/2 teaspoon ground ginger
1/8 teaspoon pepper
1 broiler-fryer chicken, cut in parts
1 tablespoon corn starch
1/4 cup cold water
Cooked rice

In small bowl stir together undrained pineapple, corn syrup, lemon juice, soy sauce, salt, ginger and pepper. Place chicken skin-side down in shallow roasting pan. Top with 1/2 of the pineapple mixture. Bake in 375°F oven 30 minutes. Turn chicken; top with remaining pineapple mixture and bake 30 minutes longer or until chicken is tender. Remove chicken to platter; keep warm. Skim fat from liquid in baking pan. Mix corn starch and water. Stir into liquid in pan. Stirring constantly, bring to boil over medium heat and boil 1 minute. Spoon sauce over chicken and serve with rice. Makes 4 servings.

FRUITED CHICKEN

1/4 cup corn oil	1/2 teaspoon salt
1 broiler-fryer chicken, cut in parts	1/4 teaspoon ground cloves
1/2 cup sliced green onion	2 tablespoons corn starch
1/4 pound mushrooms, sliced	2 tablespoons water
1 1/4 cups chicken broth	2 oranges, sectioned
1/4 cup Karo dark corn syrup	4 green-tipped bananas, split lengthwise and cut in half
3 tablespoons lemon juice	

In large skillet heat corn oil over medium-high heat. Add chicken and brown on all sides. Add onion and mushrooms; cook 5 minutes. Add broth, corn syrup, lemon juice, salt and cloves. Reduce heat. Cover and simmer about 30 minutes or until chicken is tender. Remove chicken to platter; keep warm. Mix corn starch and water until smooth. Stir into liquid in skillet. Stirring constantly, bring to boil over medium heat and boil 1 minute. Add oranges and bananas. Heat about 5 minutes or until fruit is warmed. Makes 4 servings.

EASY SESAME CHICKEN

1/3 cup Karo light corn syrup	2 tablespoons prepared mustard
2 tablespoons margarine, melted	1 teaspoon curry powder
2 tablespoons sesame seeds	1/2 teaspoon salt
	1 broiler-fryer chicken, cut in parts

In pie plate stir together corn syrup, margarine, sesame seeds, mustard, curry powder and salt. Dip chicken in syrup mixture to coat well. Place skin-side up in shallow roasting pan. Bake in 375°F oven 60 to 70 minutes or until tender. Makes 4 servings.

33

SKILLET BARBECUED CHICKEN

2	tablespoons margarine	1/2	cup catchup
1	broiler-fryer chicken, cut in parts	1	tablespoon Worcestershire sauce
1/2	cup chopped onion	1/2	teaspoon salt
1/2	cup Karo dark corn syrup		

In large skillet melt margarine over medium heat. Add chicken; brown on all sides. Drain off fat. In small bowl stir together onion, corn syrup, catchup, Worcestershire sauce and salt; pour over chicken. Cover; cook, turning frequently, 15 minutes or until chicken is tender. Uncover; continue cooking, turning frequently, 5 minutes or until glazed. Makes 4 servings.

EASY TURKEY STEW

1	can (16 oz) whole tomatoes	1/2	teaspoon salt
2	tablespoons corn oil	3	cups cooked turkey, cut in 1-inch cubes
1	cup sliced onion	1	package (10 oz) frozen peas
1	clove garlic, minced	1	piece (3 x 1-inch) orange peel
1/2	cup chicken broth	2	tablespoons corn starch
1/4	cup Karo dark corn syrup	3	tablespoons water
1/2	teaspoon dried thyme leaves		

Reserving liquid, drain and cut tomatoes in half. In large skillet heat corn oil over medium-high heat. Add onion and garlic. Sauté 5 minutes. Stir in tomatoes and liquid, chicken broth, corn syrup, thyme and salt. Bring to boil; reduce heat and simmer 15 minutes. Add turkey, peas and orange peel; simmer 10 minutes. Mix corn starch and water until smooth. Stir into turkey mixture. Stirring constantly, bring to boil over medium heat and boil 1 minute. Makes 6 servings.

GINGER FRIED SHRIMP

1 tablespoon soy sauce	1/2 cup flour
1 tablespoon dry sherry	1/3 cup corn starch
1/4 teaspoon ground cinnamon	3/4 cup water
1/4 teaspoon pepper	1 tablespoon corn oil
1/8 teaspoon ground cloves	1 egg white
1 pound large shrimp, shelled, deveined	1 quart (about) corn oil Ginger Sauce (recipe follows)

In bowl stir together soy sauce, sherry, cinnamon, pepper and cloves. Add shrimp; toss to coat well. Cover; chill while preparing batter. In large bowl stir together flour and corn starch. Gradually stir in water until smooth. Stir in 1 tablespoon corn oil. Let stand 30 minutes. In small bowl beat egg white until stiff peaks form; fold into batter. Pour corn oil into heavy 3-quart saucepan or deep fryer, filling no more than 1/3 full. Heat over medium heat to 375°F. Dip shrimp into batter and fry, a few at a time, 3 to 4 minutes or until golden. Drain on paper towels. Keep warm. Prepare Ginger Sauce. Serve shrimp with sauce. Makes 4 to 6 servings.

Ginger Sauce: In small bowl stir together 1/2 cup water, 1/4 cup Karo dark corn syrup, 2 tablespoons soy sauce, 2 tablespoons dry sherry and 1 tablespoon catchup. In large skillet heat 2 tablespoons corn oil over medium heat. Add 1/4 pound snow peas, 1/2 cup sliced water chestnuts, 1 small sweet red pepper, diced, 1 medium onion, cut in wedges, 1 clove garlic, minced and 1/2 teaspoon ground ginger. Stir fry 3 minutes or until vegetables are tender-crisp. Add sauce; bring to boil. Mix 1 tablespoon corn starch and 1 tablespoon water until smooth. Stir into sauce. Stirring constantly, bring to boil over medium heat and boil 1 minute. Makes about 2 cups.

35

SWEET AND SOUR SHRIMP

1/4 cup corn oil
1 pound medium
     shrimp, shelled,
     deveined
1 medium onion, cut in
     wedges
1 green pepper, cut in
     1-inch cubes
1 clove garlic, minced
1 teaspoon ground
     ginger

2 tablespoons corn
     starch
1 teaspoon salt
1/2 cup water
1/3 cup Karo light corn
     syrup
1/3 cup catchup
1/4 cup cider vinegar
1 can (8 oz) water chest-
     nuts, drained, sliced
     Cooked rice

In large skillet or wok heat corn oil over medium-high heat. Add shrimp. Stir fry 3 to 4 minutes or until pink. Remove shrimp. Add onion, pepper, garlic and ginger. Stirring frequently, cook about 5 minutes or until onion has browned lightly. In small bowl stir together corn starch, salt and water. Stir into onion mixture. Stir in corn syrup, catchup and vinegar. Add shrimp and water chestnuts. Stirring constantly, bring to boil over medium heat and boil 1 minute. Serve over rice. Makes 4 servings.

ALL-PURPOSE BARBECUE SAUCE

2 tablespoons corn oil
1/4 cup finely chopped
     onion
1 cup chili sauce
1/3 cup water
1/4 cup Karo dark corn
     syrup

1/4 cup cider vinegar
1 tablespoon Worcester-
     shire sauce
1/2 teaspoon salt

In saucepan heat corn oil over medium heat. Add onion; sauté 5 minutes. Stir in chili sauce, water, corn syrup, vinegar, Worcestershire sauce and salt. Bring to boil; reduce heat and simmer 10 minutes. Brush sauce on sausage, meat or poultry during last 20 minutes of cooking. Makes about 2 cups.

SAVORY BARBECUE SAUCE

2 cans (8 oz each)
tomato sauce
1/2 cup Karo dark corn
syrup
1/3 cup cider vinegar
1/4 cup minced onion

2 tablespoons prepared
mustard
2 tablespoons Worces-
tershire sauce
1 teaspoon hot pepper
sauce

In saucepan mix tomato sauce, corn syrup, vinegar, onion, mustard, Worcestershire sauce and hot pepper sauce. Bring to boil over medium heat and boil 2 minutes. Serve with meat or poultry; or brush on during last 1/2 hour of cooking. Makes 2 1/2 cups.

SPICY CRANBERRY SAUCE

2 tablespoons corn
starch
1/2 cup orange juice
1 can (16 oz) whole berry
cranberry sauce
1/2 cup Karo light or dark
corn syrup

1/4 teaspoon ground
cinnamon
1/8 teaspoon ground
cloves

In saucepan mix corn starch and orange juice until smooth. Stir in cranberry sauce, corn syrup, cinnamon and cloves. Stirring constantly, bring to boil over medium heat and boil 1 minute. Serve with chicken or ham. Makes 2 3/4 cups.

APRICOT GLAZE FOR HAM

1 can (17 oz) apricot
halves
1/2 cup Karo light or dark
corn syrup

1 teaspoon ground
ginger
1/4 teaspoon ground
cloves

In blender container place undrained apricots, corn syrup, ginger and cloves; cover. Blend on high speed 30 seconds or until smooth. Brush frequently on ham during last hour of baking. Heat remaining glaze; serve with ham. Makes about 2 cups.

FLAMING STRAWBERRY HAM GLAZE

1 (5 lb) canned
   ready-to-eat ham
1 cup sliced strawberries
6 tablespoons orange
   liqueur

1/4 cup Karo light corn
     syrup

Score ham and bake according to package directions. In saucepan stir together strawberries, 2 tablespoons of the orange liqueur and corn syrup. During last 1/2 hour of baking, spoon glaze over ham. Remove from oven; slice. Just before serving, carefully heat remaining 4 tablespoons liqueur; pour over ham and ignite. Serve flaming. Makes 12 to 15 servings.

CITRUS GLAZE

In bowl stir together 1/4 cup Karo light corn syrup, 1 tablespoon grated orange rind *or* 1 teaspoon grated lemon rind and 1/4 cup orange juice *or* 2 tablespoons lemon juice. Brush on ham or poultry occasionally during baking. Makes 1/2 cup.

CRANBERRY ORANGE RELISH

2 cups cranberries
1/2 cup sugar
1/2 cup Karo light corn
     syrup

1/2 cup golden raisins
1/4 cup orange juice
1 cup orange sections,
   cut in half

In saucepan stir together cranberries, sugar, corn syrup, raisins and orange juice. Bring to boil over medium heat; reduce heat and simmer 5 minutes or until cranberry skins pop. Remove from heat. Stir in orange sections. Cover; chill several hours. Makes 2 1/2 cups.

Tip: This relish is an ideal condiment for poultry, pork or ham and would be beautiful on a holiday buffet table.

FROZEN CRANBERRY RELISH

1 pound cranberries, washed, stems removed
1 large orange, quartered, seeded
2 small lemons, quartered, seeded

1 cup sugar
1 cup Karo light corn syrup
Peach halves, well drained

Put cranberries, orange and lemons through fine blade of food grinder. Or place in blender container; cover. Blend at medium speed until fruit is finely chopped. In large bowl stir together fruit, sugar and corn syrup until sugar is dissolved. Spoon into freezer container. Freeze about 1 hour or until slightly frozen. Spoon into peach halves or serve as relish with roast or other meats. Makes 4 cups.

Note: Relish may be prepared in advance. Store in pint jars in refrigerator. Serve chilled.

HORSERADISH SAUCE

1 1/2 cups real mayonnaise
1/4 cup prepared horse- radish, drained
2 tablespoons Karo light corn syrup
2 tablespoons dry sherry or tarragon vinegar

2 teaspoons prepared mustard
1/4 teaspoon hot pepper sauce
1/8 teaspoon salt

In bowl stir together real mayonnaise, horseradish, corn syrup, sherry, mustard, hot pepper sauce and salt. Cover; chill. Serve with sliced meats, such as tongue, ham or cold cuts. Makes 2 cups.

VEGETABLES WITH A DIFFERENCE

The abundance of American vegetables is wonderful. Whether gathered from the backyard garden, bought at a corner stand, or brought home frozen or canned, their bounty is sweet and good. But even these natural gifts from the earth can sometimes benefit from the loving touch of an ingenious cook. Vegetables can be glazed or candied with Karo, even assorted leftovers can be marinated and made to glow with it.

RED CABBAGE WITH APPLES

1/4 cup margarine	1 tablespoon salt
1/2 cup chopped onion	1 cup Burgundy wine
3 pounds red cabbage, shredded (3 qt)	2 tart apples, peeled, cored, sliced
1/3 cup Karo light corn syrup	1 cup red currant jelly
2 tablespoons cider vinegar	

In 5-quart dutch oven melt margarine over medium-high heat. Add onion. Stirring frequently, cook 3 minutes or until tender. Add cabbage, corn syrup, vinegar and salt. Stirring occasionally, cook 15 minutes. Stir in wine; bring to boil. Reduce heat and simmer 30 minutes or until cabbage is tender. Add apples and jelly. Stir until jelly is melted. Simmer 15 minutes longer. Makes 8 to 10 servings.

Top to bottom: *Basic Baked Beans* p. 43,
Orange Glazed Carrots and Celery p. 42,
Red Cabbage with Apples p. 41.

41

GLAZED ACORN SQUASH

2 medium acorn squash, halved, seeded	1 tablespoon margarine, melted
1 1/2 cups water	1/2 teaspoon ground cinnamon
1/3 cup Karo light corn syrup	Dash salt

In 13 x 9 x 2-inch baking dish place squash cut-side down. Add water. Bake in 400°F oven 30 minutes or until squash is firm. Drain water. Turn cut-side up. In small bowl stir together corn syrup, margarine, cinnamon and salt. Spoon corn syrup mixture evenly over squash. Bake in 350°F oven, basting occasionally, 15 minutes or until fork tender. Makes 4 servings.

ZUCCHINI BAKE

1/4 cup Karo light corn syrup	2 cloves garlic, minced
	Dash salt
2 tablespoons corn oil	1 pound zucchini, sliced

In 11 x 7 x 2-inch baking dish stir corn syrup, corn oil, garlic and salt. Add zucchini; toss to coat well. Bake in 375°F oven, stirring occasionally, 35 minutes or until fork tender. Makes 4 to 6 servings.

ORANGE GLAZED CARROTS AND CELERY

1/2 cup Karo light or dark corn syrup	1/4 cup orange juice
1/3 cup margarine	2 pounds carrots, cut in 2-inch pieces, cooked
1 teaspoon grated orange rind	6 ribs celery, cut in 1-inch pieces

In large skillet heat corn syrup, margarine, orange rind and juice over medium heat until margarine is melted. Stirring occasionally, cook 10 minutes or until thickened. Add carrots and celery. Stirring occasionally, cook 8 to 10 minutes or until glazed. Makes 6 to 8 servings.

BARBECUE STYLE BAKED BEANS

1 pound dried red kidney beans	1 cup chopped onion
2 quarts cold water	1 tablespoon Worcestershire sauce
2 quarts hot water	2 cloves garlic, minced
1 cup Karo light or dark corn syrup	2 teaspoons chili powder
1/4 cup firmly packed brown sugar	1 teaspoon ground ginger
1/2 cup catchup	1 teaspoon salt

Rinse beans. In 4-quart saucepan stir together beans and cold water; soak 8 hours or overnight. Drain. Add hot water to beans. Cover; bring to boil over medium heat and boil 1 hour. Drain; reserve liquid. In 3-quart casserole stir together beans, corn syrup, sugar, catchup, onion, Worcestershire sauce, garlic, chili powder, ginger, salt and 1 cup of the reserved liquid. Cover and bake in 300°F oven, stirring occasionally, 2 1/2 to 3 hours or until almost all liquid is absorbed. Makes 8 servings.

BASIC BAKED BEANS

1 pound dried navy (pea) beans	1/2 cup chili sauce
2 quarts cold water	2 teaspoons salt
2 quarts hot water	1 teaspoon dried thyme leaves
1/2 pound salt pork	1/2 teaspoon paprika
1 bay leaf	1/4 teaspoon pepper
1 cup chopped onion	
1 cup Karo light or dark corn syrup	

Rinse beans. In 4-quart saucepan stir together beans and cold water; soak 8 hours or overnight. Drain. Add hot water to beans. Stir in pork and bay leaf. Cover; bring to boil over medium heat and boil 1 hour. Drain; reserve liquid. In 3-quart casserole stir together beans, pork, onion, corn syrup, chili sauce, salt, thyme, paprika, pepper and 1 cup of the reserved liquid. Cover and bake in 300°F oven, stirring occasionally, 2 1/2 to 3 hours or until almost all liquid is absorbed. Makes 8 servings.

SWEET POTATO CASSEROLE

8 medium sweet
   potatoes, baked
1/2 cup Karo light or dark
   corn syrup
1/4 cup margarine

1 teaspoon ground
   cinnamon
1/2 teaspoon ground
   nutmeg
3/4 cup chopped walnuts

With spoon scoop pulp from potatoes; place in bowl. Stir in corn syrup, margarine, cinnamon and nutmeg. With mixer at medium speed beat potato mixture until smooth. Stir in 1/2 cup of the nuts. Spoon into 1-quart baking dish. Sprinkle with remaining 1/4 cup nuts. Bake in 350°F oven 20 to 30 minutes or until heated. Makes 8 servings.

CANDIED SWEET POTATOES

1 cup Karo dark corn
   syrup
1/2 cup firmly packed
   dark brown sugar
2 tablespoons margarine

12 medium sweet
   potatoes, cooked,
   peeled, halved
   lengthwise

In small saucepan bring corn syrup, brown sugar and margarine to boil over medium heat. Reduce heat and simmer 5 minutes. Pour 1/2 cup of the syrup into 13 x 9 x 2-inch baking dish. Arrange potatoes in syrup. Top with remaining syrup. Bake in 350°F oven, basting often, 20 minutes or until well glazed. Makes 12 servings.

SAUCY ORANGE YAMS

3 cans (17 oz each) yams,
   well drained
1 can (6 oz) frozen
   orange juice
   concentrate, thawed

1/2 cup Karo light corn
   syrup
1/4 cup firmly packed
   brown sugar
2 tablespoons margarine

In 13 x 9 x 2-inch greased baking dish arrange yams in single layer. In large skillet bring orange juice concentrate, corn syrup, sugar and margarine to boil over medium heat. Stirring frequently, boil 10 minutes or until thick and syrupy. Pour over yams. Bake in 325°F oven, basting frequently, 20 to 25 minutes or until heated. Spoon into serving dish. If desired, garnish with orange slices. Makes 12 servings.

BAKED STUFFED SWEET POTATOES

4 medium sweet potatoes	1/2 teaspoon salt
1/4 cup Karo light corn syrup	Dash ground cinnamon
1/4 cup margarine, melted	

With fork pierce each potato once and place on cookie sheet. Bake in 400°F oven 1 hour or until tender. With sharp pointed knife, cut an oval in top of each potato. Scoop out potatoes; reserve skins. In bowl mash potatoes. Add corn syrup, margarine and salt; stir until smooth. Spoon potato mixture into skins; sprinkle with cinnamon. Bake in 350°F oven 15 minutes or until heated through. Makes 4 servings.

MARINATED VEGETABLES

2 cups corn oil	1 clove garlic, minced
1/2 cup Karo light corn syrup	1/2 pound green beans, trimmed
1/2 cup lemon juice	4 carrots, sliced
2 teaspoons dried dill weed	1 pound new potatoes, sliced, cooked
2 teaspoons dried basil leaves	2 zucchini, sliced
1 teaspoon salt	1 red onion, sliced
	1 cup sliced mushrooms

In small bowl mix together corn oil, corn syrup, lemon juice, dill, basil, salt and garlic until well mixed. In 2-quart saucepan cook beans and carrots separately in boiling water 5 minutes or until tender-crisp; drain. Immediately plunge into ice water. In large shallow dish arrange beans, carrots, potatoes, zucchini, onion and mushrooms. Pour marinade over vegetables. Cover; chill several hours or overnight. Arrange vegetables on lettuce-lined platter. If desired, spoon marinade over vegetables. Makes 6 to 8 servings.

SALAD DELIGHTS

Versatile and joyful combinations in endless variety, salads are a celebration of good eating. Salads are fruits in season. They're vegetables with the glow of summer. They're hearty one-dish meals, too. Karo helps blend their many ingredients, dressing salads with sheen and grace. Karo adds smoothness to salad dressings, flavors ingredients and makes combinations harmonious and pleasing.

PERFECTION SALAD

2 envelopes unflavored gelatin	2 1/2 cups finely shredded cabbage
1 teaspoon salt	1 cup finely chopped celery
1 cup boiling water	
1/2 cup Karo light corn syrup	1/2 cup finely chopped green pepper
1 1/2 cups cold water	1/4 cup finely chopped pimiento
1/2 cup tarragon vinegar	
2 tablespoons lemon juice	

In bowl mix together gelatin and salt. Add boiling water; stir until dissolved. Stir in corn syrup, cold water, vinegar and lemon juice. Cover; chill until spoon drawn through gelatin leaves definite impression. Fold in cabbage, celery, pepper and pimiento. Spoon into 6-cup mold. Cover; chill until set. Unmold on lettuce-lined platter. Makes 10 servings.

Tip: Perfection Salad is an ideal party dish. It looks beautiful on a buffet table and can be made well ahead.

Top to bottom:
Spinach and Turkey Salad p. 48,
Perfection Salad p. 47,
German Potato Salad p. 50.

MARINATED CUCUMBERS

3 medium cucumbers, thinly sliced
2 teaspoons salt
3/4 cup tarragon vinegar

1/4 cup Karo light corn syrup
1/2 cup chopped parsley
1/4 teaspoon pepper

In large shallow dish lightly toss cucumbers and salt. In small bowl mix together vinegar, corn syrup, 1/4 cup of the parsley and pepper. Pour over cucumbers; toss to coat evenly. Cover; chill several hours or overnight. Just before serving, sprinkle with remaining parsley. Makes 8 servings.

FRUITED TUNA TOSS

5 cups torn lettuce
2 cups cubed red apple
1 cup seedless green grapes
1 can (7 oz) tuna, drained, flaked

1/3 cup chopped walnuts
1/2 cup real mayonnaise
3 tablespoons Karo dark corn syrup
4 teaspoons lemon juice
1 tablespoon soy sauce

In large salad bowl toss together lettuce, apple, grapes, tuna and nuts. In small bowl with fork stir real mayonnaise, corn syrup, lemon juice and soy sauce. Just before serving, toss with salad until coated. Makes 4 to 6 servings.

SPINACH AND TURKEY SALAD

1/2 cup corn oil
1/4 cup Karo light corn syrup
2 tablespoons white wine vinegar
1 tablespoon curry powder
1/4 teaspoon salt

2 cups cubed cooked turkey
1 orange, peeled, sectioned
1/4 cup thinly sliced red onion
6 cups torn spinach
1/2 cup chopped walnuts

In large salad bowl stir together corn oil, corn syrup, vinegar, curry powder and salt until well mixed. Add turkey, orange and onion; toss to coat well. Cover; chill at least 1 hour. Just before serving, add spinach and nuts; toss to coat. Makes 4 servings.

MARINATED BEEF SALAD

2/3 cup corn oil	1 cup sliced mushrooms
1/3 cup white wine vinegar	1 small red onion, sliced
2 tablespoons Karo dark corn syrup	8 cups torn romaine lettuce
1 tablespoon prepared horseradish, drained	2 cups torn iceberg lettuce
1 teaspoon salt	10 cherry tomatoes, cut in half
1 teaspoon dry mustard	
1/4 teaspoon pepper	
3 cups cooked lean beef strips	

In small bowl stir together corn oil, vinegar, corn syrup, horseradish, salt, mustard and pepper until well blended. Place beef, mushrooms and onion in shallow dish. Pour dressing over beef mixture. Toss to coat. Cover; chill at least 2 hours. Just before serving, toss together lettuce, tomatoes and beef mixture. Makes 6 servings.

WALDORF SLAW

1 cup real mayonnaise	1 can (11 oz) mandarin orange sections, drained
1/2 cup Karo light corn syrup	
1 tablespoon lemon juice	2 cups diced red apple
1/4 teaspoon salt	1/2 cup raisins
2 quarts shredded cabbage (about 2 lb)	1/4 cup coarsely chopped walnuts
1 can (8 oz) pineapple chunks, drained	

In small bowl mix together real mayonnaise, corn syrup, lemon juice and salt. Chill. In large bowl toss together cabbage, pineapple, oranges, apple and raisins. Just before serving, toss with dressing. Garnish with nuts. Makes 12 servings.

GERMAN POTATO SALAD

12 slices bacon
1 cup sliced onion
1 cup sliced celery
1/4 cup Karo dark corn syrup
3 tablespoons cider vinegar
1 teaspoon salt
1/4 teaspoon pepper
3 pounds potatoes, cooked, peeled, sliced (6 cups)

In skillet fry bacon over medium-high heat until crisp. Drain on paper towels. Pour off all but 2 tablespoons drippings. Add onion. Stirring occasionally, cook 2 minutes. Add celery; cook 3 minutes or until tender-crisp. Stir in corn syrup, vinegar, salt and pepper. Bring to boil and boil 1 minute. Crumble bacon; add to potatoes. Pour dressing over potato mixture; toss to coat well. Serve warm or chilled. Makes 8 to 10 servings.

CHINESE HAM SALAD

1/4 cup corn oil
2 tablespoons Karo light corn syrup
2 tablespoons soy sauce
1/4 teaspoon ground ginger
1/8 teaspoon pepper
2 cups cooked julienne ham
2 cups cooked rice
1 can (8 oz) water chestnuts, drained, sliced
1/2 cup slivered green pepper
1/2 cup shredded carrot
1/4 cup chopped onion

In large bowl stir together corn oil, corn syrup, soy sauce, ginger and pepper. Add ham, rice, water chestnuts, green pepper, carrot and onion. Toss to coat well. Cover; chill at least 1 hour. Makes 4 servings.

POPPY SEED DRESSING

2/3 cup orange juice
1/2 cup Karo light corn
    syrup

1/2 cup corn oil
1 tablespoon poppy
    seeds

In jar place orange juice, corn syrup, corn oil and poppy seeds. Cover tightly; shake well. Chill. Shake before serving. Serve with fruit salad or mixed greens. Makes 1 1/2 cups.

CREAMY DRESSING

1/2 cup real mayonnaise
1/2 cup dairy sour cream
1/4 cup Karo light corn
    syrup

1/4 teaspoon ground
    nutmeg

In small bowl stir together real mayonnaise, sour cream, corn syrup and nutmeg until smooth. Serve with fruit salad. Makes about 1 cup.

Raspberry Dressing: Follow recipe for Creamy Dressing. Add 3/4 cup fresh or thawed, drained frozen red raspberries. Serve with fruit salad. Makes about 2 cups.

Cucumber Dressing: Follow recipe for Creamy Dressing. Omit nutmeg. Add 1/2 cup pared, chopped, drained cucumber and 2 tablespoons drained horseradish. Serve over salad greens. Makes about 2 cups.

Tip: This is a dressing for all seasons. Use it on summer berries or melon or a winter combination of apples, bananas and oranges. Sprinkle with nuts if desired.

51

DESSERTS TO REMEMBER

More than in any other part of the meal, dessert time provides the cook with an opportunity to create something beautiful, wonderful, mouthwatering to recall. It is an opportunity to make the most of seasonal fruits, to explore the cooking heritage of ancestral homelands, or to create new memories and original traditions. A fine dessert says, "I love you." Yet with today's easy cooking methods and such helps as Karo corn syrup, dessert making is no chore. In fact, it's a joy.

PLUM KUCHEN

1 1/4	cups unsifted flour	1	egg, slightly beaten
1/4	cup sugar	1	teaspoon vanilla
1 1/4	teaspoons baking powder	1 1/2	pounds plums, sliced
1	teaspoon ground cinnamon	1/4	cup margarine, melted
1/4	cup margarine	1/4	cup Karo light corn syrup
1/3	cup Karo light corn syrup		

Grease 13 x 9 x 2-inch baking pan. In bowl stir together flour, sugar, baking powder and cinnamon. With pastry blender or 2 knives cut in margarine until fine crumbs form. Add 1/3 cup corn syrup, egg and vanilla. Beat vigorously until smooth. Spread batter in prepared pan. Arrange plums in 3 rows on top. In small bowl stir together melted margarine and 1/4 cup corn syrup. Brush plums with mixture. Bake in 400°F oven 35 minutes or until golden and fruit is tender. Serve warm with ice cream. Makes 12 servings.

Top to bottom: *Deluxe Pecan Pie* p. 63,
Easy Frozen Yogurt p. 75 with *Strawberry Sauce* p. 60, *Pear Dumplings* p. 54.

PEAR DUMPLINGS

1/4 cup raisins
1/4 cup Karo light corn syrup
2 tablespoons margarine, melted
1/2 teaspoon ground cinnamon
1 recipe double crust pastry

4 small pears, peeled, cored
1 cup Karo light corn syrup
1 cup shredded coconut
3 tablespoons water
2 tablespoons margarine

Grease 13 x 9 x 2-inch baking pan. In small bowl stir together raisins, corn syrup, 2 tablespoons margarine and cinnamon. On lightly floured surface roll out pastry, 1/4 at a time to 7 1/2-inch square. Use pastry wheel for decorative edge. Place a pear in center of each square. Fill center of pear with 2 tablespoons of raisin mixture. Moisten edges of pastry; bring corners to top of pear. Pinch edges together firmly to cover pear. Place dumplings in prepared pan. Cut remaining pastry into small leaves; moisten edge; press two on top of each pear. Bake in 425°F oven 40 minutes or until lightly browned. In 1-quart saucepan stir together corn syrup, coconut, water and 2 tablespoons margarine over medium-high heat until boiling. Pour over dumplings during last 5 minutes of baking, basting occasionally. Serve immediately with remaining sauce. Makes 4 servings.

SPICED BAKED APPLES

4 medium baking apples, cored
1/2 cup Karo light or dark corn syrup
1/4 cup margarine, melted
1/4 cup firmly packed brown sugar

1 teaspoon ground cinnamon
1 teaspoon vanilla
1/4 teaspoon ground nutmeg

Starting from stem end, peel apples 1/3 of the way down; place in 8 x 8 x 2-inch baking dish. In bowl stir together corn syrup, margarine, sugar, cinnamon, vanilla and nutmeg; spoon over apples. Bake in 350°F oven 45 minutes basting often, or until tender. Makes 4 servings.

LEMON PEAR MERINGUE

1 cup Karo light corn
   syrup
   Peel from 1 lemon
1/4 cup lemon juice
2 tablespoons margarine
3 pears, peeled, halved,
   cored

3 tablespoons toasted
   slivered almonds
2 egg whites
1/4 cup Karo light corn
   syrup

In 10-inch skillet stir together 1 cup corn syrup, lemon peel and lemon juice. Stirring frequently, bring to boil over medium heat and boil 2 minutes. Stir in margarine until melted. Add pears. Reduce heat. Simmer, turning and basting frequently 10 minutes or until tender. Arrange pears, cut side up, in 8 or 9-inch pie plate. Pour lemon mixture over pears. Spoon 1 teaspoon almonds into each pear cavity. In small bowl with mixer at high speed beat egg whites until foamy. Slowly beat in 1/4 cup corn syrup; continue beating until stiff peaks form. Pipe or spoon meringue over pears. Garnish with remaining almonds. Bake in 425°F oven 5 minutes or until lightly browned. Makes 6 servings.

PLUM-NUT COBBLER

3/4 cup Karo light corn
   syrup
1/4 cup sugar
1 tablespoon corn starch
1/2 teaspoon ground
   cinnamon
2 pounds ripe plums,
   sliced

1 1/4 cups buttermilk
   baking mix
1/2 cup finely chopped
   nuts
1/3 cup milk
1/4 cup sugar

In large bowl stir together corn syrup, 1/4 cup sugar, corn starch and cinnamon. Add plums, toss to coat well. Spoon into 8 x 8 x 2-inch baking dish. Bake in 400°F oven 15 minutes; remove from oven. In bowl stir together buttermilk baking mix, nuts, milk and 1/4 cup sugar until well blended. Beat vigorously 20 strokes. Drop by spoonfuls over fruit. Bake 15 to 20 minutes or until golden. Makes 6 servings.

PEACH COBBLER

1/2 cup Karo light corn syrup	1 cup buttermilk baking mix
1 tablespoon corn starch	1/4 cup milk
1/2 teaspoon ground cinnamon	2 tablespoons margarine, melted
6 cups sliced peeled peaches	1 tablespoon sugar

In bowl stir together corn syrup, corn starch and cinnamon. Add peaches; toss to coat well. Spoon into 8 x 8 x 2-inch baking dish. Bake in 400°F oven 15 minutes; remove from oven. In bowl stir together buttermilk baking mix, milk, margarine and sugar until smooth. Beat vigorously 20 strokes. Drop by spoonfuls over fruit. Bake 15 to 20 minutes or until golden. Makes 6 servings.

STEWED RHUBARB

3/4 cup Karo light corn syrup	3 1/2 cups cut-up rhubarb (1 lb)
1/4 cup sugar	

In 2-quart saucepan stir together corn syrup and sugar until well mixed. Add rhubarb. Stirring constantly, bring to boil over medium heat. Boil 3 to 5 minutes or until rhubarb is soft. Serve warm or chilled. Makes 2 1/2 cups.

CANTALOUPE CREAM SOUP

3 pounds cantaloupe, seeded, peeled, cut-up (3 cups)	2 tablespoons lime or lemon juice
1/2 cup Karo light corn syrup	1/2 cup heavy cream

Place cantaloupe, corn syrup and juice in blender container; cover. Blend on high speed 30 seconds. Add cream; cover. Blend 30 seconds or until smooth. Cover; chill several hours. Stir before serving. Garnish with whipped cream. Makes 4 to 5 servings.

HOT FRUIT COMPOTE

1/2 cup sugar
1/2 teaspoon ground
       ginger
1/2 teaspoon ground
       nutmeg
  2 pears, peeled, cored,
       sliced
  2 apples, peeled, cored,
       sliced
  1 cup peach slices

1/2 cup dried apricots
1/2 cup pitted prunes
       Peel from 1 lemon
  3 tablespoons lemon
       juice
  1 (3-inch) cinnamon
       stick
1/2 cup Karo light corn
       syrup

In small bowl mix together sugar, ginger and nutmeg. In 2-quart casserole place pears, apples, peaches, apricots, prunes, lemon peel and lemon juice. Add sugar mixture; toss to coat well. Add cinnamon stick. Cover. Stirring occasionally, bake in 325°F oven 1 hour or until fruit is soft. Stir in corn syrup. Cover; let stand 10 to 15 minutes. Serve warm. Makes 6 to 8 servings.

Tip: Frozen peach slices, thawed, may be substituted for fresh peaches.

STRAWBERRY CREAM

  1 pint strawberries,
       hulled
1/2 cup Karo light corn
       syrup
1/2 cup raspberry jam
  1 tablespoon lemon
       juice

1/4 cup water
  1 envelope unflavored
       gelatin
  1 cup heavy cream,
       whipped

Place strawberries, corn syrup, jam and lemon juice in blender container; cover. Blend on high speed 1 minute or until smooth. Pour into bowl. In small saucepan stir water and gelatin. Stir constantly over very low heat until dissolved. Stir into strawberry mixture. Chill 1 hour or until mixture begins to thicken. Fold in half of the whipped cream. Spoon into dessert cups. Cover; chill 2 hours or until set. Just before serving, garnish with remaining whipped cream. Makes 6 servings.

RHUBARB STRAWBERRY DESSERT

1 pound rhubarb, cut in 1-inch pieces (about 3 cups)	3/4 cup Karo light corn syrup
1 pint strawberries, hulled, quartered	2 eggs
5 tablespoons corn starch	2 cups unsifted flour
1 cup Karo light corn syrup	1 tablespoon baking powder
1/3 cup margarine	1 teaspoon salt
1/4 cup sugar	3/4 cup milk
	Topping (recipe follows)

In 2-quart saucepan toss together rhubarb, strawberries and corn starch. Stir in 1 cup corn syrup. Stirring constantly, bring to boil over medium heat and boil 1 minute. Cool. Grease 13 x 9 x 2-inch baking pan. In large bowl with mixer at low speed beat margarine until soft. With mixer at medium speed beat in sugar until well blended. Slowly pour in 3/4 cup corn syrup; beat until well blended. Add eggs, one at a time, beating well after each addition. In small bowl stir together flour, baking powder and salt. At low speed add flour mixture in 3 additions alternately with milk, beginning and ending with flour. Beat after each addition until batter is smooth. Spread one half of the batter in prepared pan. Cover with rhubarb mixture. Top with remaining batter. Sprinkle with Topping. Bake in 350°F oven 40 to 45 minutes or until cake tester inserted in center comes out clean. Makes 12 servings.

Topping: In bowl stir together 3/4 cup sugar, 1/2 cup unsifted flour and 1 teaspoon ground cinnamon. With pastry blender or 2 knives cut in 1/4 cup margarine until crumbs form.

FLAVORFUL SAUCES

Dessert sauces almost fall into the category of magic. With scarcely any effort at all they turn a simple cake, an easy custard, a dish of ice cream, a bowl of fruit, even a ready-prepared dessert, into a culinary triumph.

BLUEBERRY SAUCE

1 1/2 cups fresh blueberries
  1/2 cup Karo light
      corn syrup

In blender container place blueberries and corn syrup; cover. Blend on high speed 1 minute or until smooth. Makes about 2 cups.

GRAPE SAUCE

1/2 cup grape jam
  1 cup Karo light
     corn syrup

In bowl stir jam until smooth. Stir in corn syrup until well blended. Makes about 1 cup.

PINEAPPLE SAUCE

1 can (8 oz) crushed
   pineapple in own
   juice

1 cup Karo light
   corn syrup

Place pineapple and corn syrup in blender container; cover. Blend at high speed 10 seconds or until fairly smooth. Makes about 2 cups.

STRAWBERRY SAUCE

1 package (10 oz) frozen strawberries in syrup, thawed	1 cup Karo light corn syrup

Drain strawberries reserving liquid; mash until fairly smooth. Stir in corn syrup and enough reserved liquid to obtain desired consistency. Makes 1 2/3 cups.

Raspberry Sauce: Follow recipe for Strawberry Sauce. Substitute 1 package (10 oz) frozen raspberries for strawberries.

CRANAPPLE SAUCE

1 cup cranberries	1/2 cup Karo light corn syrup
1 cup chopped, peeled apple	1 teaspoon grated orange rind
1/2 cup sugar	

In saucepan bring cranberries, apple, sugar and corn syrup to boil over medium heat. Reduce heat and simmer 5 minutes or until cranberries pop. Stir in orange rind. Makes 1 3/4 cups.

APRICOT SAUCE

1 cup water	1 cup Karo light corn syrup
1/3 cup dried apricots	

In saucepan bring water and apricots to boil over medium heat. Cover; cook 10 minutes or until apricots are tender. Mash until fairly smooth. Stir in corn syrup. Cool. Makes about 2 cups.

JUBILEE SAUCE

1 can (16 1/2 oz) pitted
   dark, sweet cherries
   packed in water
1/2 cup Karo light
   corn syrup

2 tablespoons corn
   starch
1/4 cup brandy

Drain and reserve liquid from cherries. In saucepan, gradually stir reserved cherry liquid and corn syrup into corn starch until smooth. Stirring constantly, bring to boil over medium heat and boil 1 minute. Remove from heat; stir in cherries and brandy. Serve warm. Makes about 2 1/2 cups.

FUDGY PEANUT BUTTER SAUCE

1/2 cup Karo light
   corn syrup
1/2 cup creamy
   peanut butter

1/2 cup chocolate-flavored
   syrup

In bowl stir corn syrup, peanut butter and chocolate syrup until smooth. Makes 1 3/4 cups.

CINNAMON SAUCE

1 cup sugar
1/2 cup Karo light corn
   syrup
1/4 cup water

1/2 teaspoon ground
   cinnamon
1/2 cup evaporated milk

In saucepan stir together sugar, corn syrup, water and cinnamon. Stirring constantly, bring to boil over medium heat and boil 2 minutes. Remove from heat. Stir in evaporated milk. Cool. Makes 1 1/3 cups.

SPICED RAISIN SAUCE

1 cup raisins	2 tablespoons corn starch
1 cup Karo dark corn syrup	2 tablespoons water
1/2 cup water	1/4 cup dark rum
1/2 teaspoon ground cinnamon	1/4 teaspoon vanilla
1/8 teaspoon ground nutmeg	

In saucepan stir together raisins, corn syrup, 1/2 cup water, cinnamon and nutmeg. Bring to boil over medium heat. Cover; simmer 10 minutes. Mix corn starch and 2 tablespoons water until smooth. Add to syrup mixture. Stirring constantly, bring to boil over medium heat and boil 1 minute. Remove from heat; stir in rum and vanilla. Serve warm. Makes about 2 cups.

OLD FASHIONED HOT FUDGE SAUCE

1 cup sugar	2 1/2 cups evaporated milk
1 cup Karo light corn syrup	3 tablespoons margarine
1/2 cup unsweetened cocoa	1/4 teaspoon salt
	1 teaspoon vanilla

In heavy 2-quart saucepan mix together sugar, corn syrup, cocoa, milk, margarine and salt. Stirring constantly, bring to boil over medium heat. Stirring occasionally, boil 3 minutes. Remove from heat. Stir in vanilla. Serve warm. Makes 2 1/2 cups.

FAMOUS PIES

Pecan pie, the grand American original that in some parts of this country is still known as Karo pie, is the most celebrated member of a whole family of outstanding dessert pies made delicious, glowing and smooth with Karo corn syrup.

DELUXE PECAN PIE

3 eggs	1 teaspoon vanilla
1 cup Karo light or dark corn syrup	1/8 teaspoon salt
1 cup sugar	1 cup pecans
2 tablespoons margarine, melted	1 unbaked (9-inch) pastry shell

In medium bowl with mixer at medium speed beat eggs slightly. Beat in corn syrup, sugar, margarine, vanilla and salt. Stir in nuts. Pour into pastry shell. Bake in 350°F oven 55 to 65 minutes or until knife inserted halfway between center and edge comes out clean. Cool. Makes 8 servings.

Date Nut Pie: Follow recipe for Deluxe Pecan Pie. Substitute 1 cup finely chopped dates and 1/2 cup walnut halves for pecans.

Fudge Nut Pie: Follow recipe for Deluxe Pecan Pie. Melt 2 squares (1 oz each) unsweetened chocolate with margarine. Reduce eggs to 2.

Meringue Pecan Pie: Follow recipe for Deluxe Pecan Pie. Coarsely chop pecans. Cool. In small bowl with mixer at high speed beat 3 eggs whites until foamy. Gradually add 1/3 cup corn syrup. Continue beating until stiff peaks form. Spread over filling sealing to edge of crust. Bake in 425°F oven 5 minutes or until lightly browned. Cool at room temperature away from drafts.

AMBROSIA PIZZA

1 frozen (9-inch) extra deep pie shell	1 cup cold milk
1 package (8 oz) cream cheese	1 package (3 3/4 oz) instant vanilla pudding mix
1 tablespoon grated orange rind	1 cup toasted coconut
1/2 cup Karo light corn syrup	1 orange, peeled, sliced
	1/4 cup seedless green grapes, halved

Remove pastry shell from pie pan. Place on cookie sheet to thaw. With hands flatten and shape into 12-inch circle. Flute edge. Pierce with fork. Bake in 425°F oven 10 to 12 minutes or until lightly browned. In large bowl with mixer at high speed beat cream cheese until smooth. Add orange rind; beat until well mixed. While beating, slowly pour in corn syrup; beat until light and fluffy. In small bowl with mixer at low speed beat milk and pudding mix 2 minutes. Fold into cream cheese mixture. Spoon onto prepared crust. Sprinkle with coconut. Arrange oranges and grapes on top. Cover with plastic wrap; chill. Makes 8 to 10 servings.

STRAWBERRY PARFAIT PIE

1 pint strawberries, hulled, quartered	1 packaged (6 oz) graham cracker crust
1 cup Karo light corn syrup	Whipped cream
1 quart vanilla ice cream	

In 2-quart saucepan bring strawberries and corn syrup to boil over medium heat. Boil 7 to 8 minutes or until mixture is thickened and reduced by one half. Cool completely. In large bowl with mixer at medium-low speed, beat ice cream to soften. Spoon 1/3 of ice cream into crust. Drizzle with 1/3 of strawberry sauce. Repeat ending with ice cream. Smooth with spatula. Cover; freeze until firm. Before serving, top with whipped cream. Serve with remaining strawberry sauce. Makes 8 servings.

VELVETY PUMPKIN PIE

1 can (16 oz) mashed,
   cooked pumpkin
1 cup Karo light or dark
   corn syrup
2/3 cup evaporated milk
3 eggs, separated
2 envelopes unflavored
   gelatin

2 teaspoons pumpkin
   pie spice
1/4 cup firmly packed
   brown sugar
1 baked (9-inch)
   graham cracker
   crust

In heavy 2-quart saucepan stir together pumpkin, corn syrup, evaporated milk, egg yolks, gelatin and pumpkin pie spice until smooth. Stirring constantly with wire whisk, cook over medium-low heat just until mixture boils and thickens. Chill until mixture mounds when dropped from spoon. In small bowl with mixer at high speed beat egg whites until foamy. Gradually beat in sugar; continue beating until stiff peaks form. Gently fold into pumpkin mixture. Spoon into crust. Chill at least 2 hours or until set. Makes 8 servings.

CHOCOLATE ALMOND PIE

3 eggs
1 cup Karo light or dark
   corn syrup
1/2 cup sugar
2 tablespoons
   margarine, melted
1 teaspoon vanilla

1/4 teaspoon salt
1/2 cup semisweet
   chocolate pieces
1/2 cup sliced almonds
1 unbaked (9-inch)
   pastry shell

In bowl with fork beat eggs slightly. Beat in corn syrup, sugar, margarine, vanilla and salt until well blended. Stir in chocolate pieces and nuts. Pour into pastry shell. Bake in 350°F oven 50 to 60 minutes or until knife inserted halfway between center and edge comes out clean. Cool. If desired, serve with whipped cream. Makes 8 servings.

CHOCOLATE WALNUT PIE

2 eggs, slightly beaten	1 teaspoon vanilla
1 1/2 cups Karo light corn syrup	1/8 teaspoon salt
4 squares (1 oz each) semisweet chocolate, melted	1 cup coarsely chopped walnuts
2 tablespoons margarine, melted	1 unbaked (9-inch) pastry shell
2 tablespoons corn starch	

In large bowl stir together eggs, corn syrup, chocolate, margarine, corn starch, vanilla and salt. Stir in nuts. Pour into pastry shell. Bake in 350°F oven 45 minutes. (Do not over bake. Filling should be slightly less set in center.) Cool. Makes 8 servings.

PEACH CRUMB PIE

1 cup unsifted flour	1/2 cup Karo light corn syrup
1/2 cup firmly packed brown sugar	4 1/2 cups peeled, sliced peaches or nectarines (about 2 lb)
1/2 cup margarine	
1/2 cup chopped walnuts	
3 tablespoons corn starch	1 unbaked (9-inch) pastry shell
1/2 teaspoon ground ginger	

In bowl stir together flour and sugar. With pastry blender or 2 knives cut in margarine until crumbs form. Stir in nuts; set aside. In medium bowl mix corn starch and ginger. Stir in corn syrup until smooth. Add peaches. Toss to coat. Spoon into pastry shell. Sprinkle crumb mixture on top. Bake in 375°F oven 55 minutes or until golden brown. Makes 8 servings.

DEEP DISH PEACH PIE

1/2 cup firmly packed light
   brown sugar
3 tablespoons corn
   starch
1/4 teaspoon salt
1/2 cup Karo light corn
   syrup

5 cups sliced, peeled,
   peaches (about 3 lb)
2 tablespoons margarine
   Pastry (recipe follows)

In large bowl mix together sugar, corn starch and salt. Stir
in corn syrup. Add peaches; toss to coat well. Turn into 10 x
6 x 2-inch baking dish or 1 1/2-quart casserole. Dot with
margarine. On lightly floured surface roll out pastry 1/4 inch
larger in each direction than baking dish. Cut slits to allow
steam to escape. Place pastry over peaches. Seal and flute
edge. Bake in 425°F oven 40 minutes or until crust is brown.
Makes 6 servings.

Pastry: In medium bowl mix 1 1/4 cups unsifted flour and
1/8 teaspoon salt. With pastry blender or two knives cut in
1/2 cup margarine until fine crumbs form. Sprinkle 2 tablespoons water over mixture while tossing to blend well. Shape
into ball.

MINCEMEAT PIE

3 eggs
1 package (9 oz)
   condensed mince-
   meat, broken up
1/2 cup Karo light or dark
   corn syrup
1/4 cup margarine

1/2 cup coarsely chopped
   pecans
1 tablespoon grated
   orange rind
1 unbaked (9-inch)
   pastry shell
1/4 cup dry sherry

In bowl beat eggs slightly; set aside. In 2-quart saucepan stir
together mincemeat, corn syrup and margarine. Stirring
constantly, bring to boil over medium heat. Remove from
heat. Gradually stir into eggs. Add nuts and orange rind.
Pour into pastry shell. Bake in 350°F oven 40 to 50 minutes
or until knife inserted halfway between center and edge comes
out clean. Pour sherry over top. Cool. Makes 8 servings.

CRANAPPLE MERINGUE PIE

1 cup sugar	2 cups cranberries
1/2 cup Karo light corn syrup	1/4 cup corn starch
	3 tablespoons water
1/2 cup water	1 baked (9-inch) pastry shell
1/2 teaspoon ground cinnamon	2 egg whites
3 green apples, peeled, cut in 1/2-inch cubes (3 cups)	1/4 cup Karo light corn syrup

In saucepan stir sugar, 1/2 cup corn syrup, 1/2 cup water and cinnamon. Add apples. Cook over medium-high heat 10 minutes. Add cranberries and cook 10 minutes longer or until cranberry skins pop. Mix corn starch and 3 tablespoons water until smooth. Add to cranberry mixture. Stirring constantly, bring to boil over medium heat and boil 1 minute. Spoon into pastry shell. Cool. In small bowl with mixer at high speed beat egg whites until soft peaks form. Gradually beat in 1/4 cup corn syrup; continue beating until stiff peaks form. Pipe meringue in lattice fashion over cranberry mixture. Bake in 425°F oven 3 to 5 minutes or until meringue is brown. Makes 8 servings.

GOLDEN SYRUP WALNUT PIE

3 eggs	1/8 teaspoon salt
1 1/2 cups Karo light corn syrup	1 cup coarsely chopped walnuts
2 tablespoons margarine, melted	1 unbaked (9-inch) pastry shell
1 teaspoon vanilla	

In bowl with fork beat eggs slightly. Beat in corn syrup, margarine, vanilla and salt until well blended. Stir in nuts. Pour into pastry shell. Bake in 350°F oven 1 hour or until knife inserted halfway between center and edge comes out clean. Cool. Makes 8 servings.

OATMEAL PIE

3 eggs	1 teaspoon vanilla
1 cup Karo light or dark corn syrup	1/4 teaspoon salt
1/2 cup sugar	3/4 cup quick oats
2 tablespoons margarine, melted	1 unbaked (9-inch) pastry shell

In bowl with fork beat eggs slightly. Beat in corn syrup, sugar, margarine, vanilla and salt until well blended. Stir in oats. Pour into pastry shell. Bake in 350°F oven 45 to 55 minutes or until knife inserted halfway between center and edge comes out clean. Cool. Makes 8 servings.

RAISIN NUT PIE

3 eggs	1/4 teaspoon salt
3/4 cup Karo dark corn syrup	1 cup raisins
1/2 cup firmly packed light brown sugar	1/2 cup chopped pecans or walnuts
1/4 cup margarine, melted	1 unbaked (9-inch) pastry shell
1 teaspoon vanilla	

In bowl with fork beat eggs slightly. Beat in corn syrup, brown sugar, margarine, vanilla and salt until well blended. Stir in raisins and nuts. Pour into pastry shell. Bake in 350°F oven 40 to 50 minutes or until knife inserted halfway between center and edge comes out clean. Cool. Makes 8 servings.

MACAROON PIE

3 eggs	1/8 teaspoon salt
1 cup Karo light	1 can (3 1/2 oz) flaked
corn syrup	coconut
1/2 cup sugar	1 cup sliced almonds
2 tablespoons	1 unbaked (9-inch)
margarine, melted	pastry shell
1/4 teaspoon almond	
extract	

In bowl with fork beat eggs slightly. Beat in corn syrup, sugar, margarine, almond extract and salt until well blended. Stir in coconut and nuts. Pour into pastry shell. Bake in 350°F oven 50 to 55 minutes or until knife inserted halfway between center and edge comes out clean. Cool. Makes 8 servings.

Tip: Delicious and tempting as it is, this pie becomes even more spectacular when piped with whipped cream flavored with vanilla.

CRANBERRY WALNUT PIE

3 eggs	3/4 cup coarsely chopped
1 cup Karo light	walnuts
corn syrup	1 tablespoon grated
2/3 cup sugar	orange rind
2 tablespoons	1 unbaked (9-inch)
margarine, melted	pastry shell
1/8 teaspoon salt	
1 cup cranberries,	
chopped	

In bowl with fork beat eggs slightly. Beat in corn syrup, sugar, margarine and salt until well blended. Gently stir in cranberries, nuts and orange rind. Turn into pastry shell. Bake in 350°F oven about 1 hour or until knife inserted halfway between center and edge comes out clean. Cool. Makes 8 servings.

70

LEMON CHIFFON PIE

1 envelope unflavored gelatin	1 teaspoon grated lemon rind
1/4 cup cold water	1/2 cup lemon juice
3 eggs, separated	1/4 cup sugar
3/4 cup Karo light corn syrup	1 baked (9-inch) graham cracker crust

In heavy 2-quart saucepan sprinkle gelatin over water. Stir in egg yolks, corn syrup, lemon rind and lemon juice. Stirring constantly, cook over low heat until slightly thickened (do not boil). Cool. In small bowl with mixer at high speed beat egg whites until soft peaks form. Gradually beat in sugar; continue beating until stiff peaks form. Fold into yolk mixture. Spoon into crust. Chill until firm. Makes 8 servings.

Lime Chiffon Pie: Follow recipe for Lemon Chiffon Pie. Substitute 1 teaspoon lime rind for 1 teaspoon lemon rind and 1/2 cup lime juice for 1/2 cup lemon juice.

PEANUT BUTTER CHIFFON PIE

1 cup Karo dark corn syrup	3 eggs, separated
1/2 cup super chunk peanut butter	1 teaspoon vanilla
1/2 cup water	3 tablespoons sugar
1 envelope unflavored gelatin	1 packaged (6 oz) chocolate cookie crust
	Whipped cream

In medium saucepan stir together corn syrup, peanut butter, water, gelatin and egg yolks until well blended. Stirring constantly, cook over medium heat until thickened. Stir in vanilla. Cool until mixture mounds slightly when dropped from a spoon. In small bowl with mixer at high speed beat egg whites until soft peaks form. Gradually beat in sugar; continue beating until stiff peaks form. Carefully fold in peanut butter mixture. Chill until mixture mounds. Pile into crust; chill until firm. Garnish with whipped cream. Makes 8 servings.

71

FROZEN DESSERTS

Frosty sherbets, yogurts and ice creams are cool and scrumptious. They capture the beauty of fruit or the richness of good flavors in the most refreshing desserts of all. And they're incredibly easy to make.

FROZEN PUMPKIN PIE

1 cup mashed, cooked pumpkin	1/4 teaspoon ground cinnamon
1/2 cup Karo dark corn syrup	1 cup heavy cream
1/2 teaspoon salt	1/4 cup sugar
1/2 teaspoon ground ginger	1 baked (9-inch) graham cracker crust
1/4 teaspoon ground nutmeg	1 pint vanilla ice cream, softened

In bowl stir together pumpkin, corn syrup, salt, ginger, nutmeg and cinnamon. Whip cream, gradually beating in sugar. Fold pumpkin mixture into whipped cream. Spread bottom of crust with ice cream; spoon pumpkin mixture over ice cream. Freeze at least 2 hours. Remove from freezer 10 minutes before serving. Makes 8 servings.

FROZEN PECAN PIE

1 package (8 oz) cream cheese, softened	1 cup milk
3/4 cup Karo light corn syrup	1 teaspoon vanilla
	1 cup chopped pecans
1/4 cup firmly packed brown sugar	1 baked (9-inch) graham cracker crust

In large bowl with mixer at high speed beat cream cheese, corn syrup and sugar until smooth. With mixer at medium speed add milk and vanilla and beat until blended. Stir in nuts. Turn into crust. Freeze 6 hours or until firm. Remove from freezer 15 minutes before serving. Makes 8 servings.

VANILLA ICE CREAM

1 cup sugar	4 eggs
1/4 cup corn starch	1 quart light cream
1 teaspoon salt	2 tablespoons vanilla
1 quart milk	
1 cup Karo light corn syrup	

In heavy 3-quart saucepan stir together sugar, corn starch and salt. Gradually stir in milk and corn syrup until smooth. Stirring constantly, bring to boil over medium heat and boil 1 minute; remove from heat. In bowl beat eggs slightly. Gradually stir 1 cup mixture into eggs, then stir back into remaining hot mixture. Stirring constantly, cook over low heat until mixture thickens and coats a metal spoon (do not boil). Remove from heat and continue stirring 1 minute. Cover surface with plastic wrap or waxed paper to prevent skin from forming; refrigerate about 4 hours or until well chilled. Stir in light cream and vanilla. Freeze in 4 or 6-quart ice cream freezer following manufacturer's directions. Makes about 1 gallon.

PRALINE ICE CREAM

2 eggs, slightly beaten	1/2 cup firmly packed brown sugar
2 cups light cream or milk	1/4 teaspoon salt
1/2 cup Karo dark corn syrup	1/2 cup chopped pecans
	1 1/2 teaspoons vanilla

In heavy 2-quart saucepan stir together eggs, cream, corn syrup, sugar and salt. Stirring constantly, cook over low heat until mixture thickens and coats a metal spoon (do not boil) about 20 minutes. Remove from heat and continue stirring 1 minute. Stir in nuts and vanilla. Pour into 9 x 9 x 2-inch baking pan. Cover; freeze overnight. Soften slightly at room temperature. Spoon into large bowl. With mixer at low speed beat until smooth but not melted. Immediately return to pan. Cover; freeze until firm. Makes about 1 quart.

Tip: For a special dessert, serve Praline Ice Cream in a stemmed glass. Top with warm Cinnamon Sauce and add a few whole pecans.

PEACH ICE CREAM

2 pounds (about) fully ripe peaches	3 cups milk
	1 cup heavy cream
3/4 cup sugar	2/3 cup Karo light corn syrup
1 tablespoon lemon juice	
2 eggs	1 teaspoon vanilla

Peel, pit and finely chop peaches in food chopper, blender or processor. Stir in 1/4 cup of the sugar and lemon juice; set aside. In large bowl with mixer at medium speed beat eggs until light and frothy. Gradually add remaining 1/2 cup of sugar, beating until dissolved. Add milk, cream, corn syrup and vanilla, beating until blended. Stir in peach mixture. Freeze in 4-quart ice cream freezer following manufacturer's directions. Makes about 2 quarts.

CRUNCHY ICE CREAM TORTE

2/3 cup Karo light corn syrup	4 cups crisp rice cereal
	1 cup slivered almonds
2/3 cup super chunk peanut butter	1 quart vanilla ice cream, softened

Grease 9 x 3-inch springform pan. In large bowl stir together corn syrup and peanut butter until well mixed. Stir in cereal and nuts just until moistened. Press 3 cups of the mixture into bottom of pan. Cover with ice cream; smooth top. Freeze 1 hour or until firm. Press remaining cereal mixture evenly over ice cream. Cover; freeze until firm. Makes 8 to 10 servings.

FROSTY CANTALOUPE SHERBET

1 envelope unflavored gelatin	3 cups cubed cantaloupe
	1 cup Karo light corn syrup
1/2 cup milk	

In small saucepan sprinkle gelatin over milk. Stir constantly over low heat until dissolved. Place in blender container with cantaloupe and corn syrup; cover. Blend on high speed 30 seconds. Pour into 9 x 9 x 2-inch baking pan. Cover; freeze overnight. Soften slightly at room temperature. Spoon into large bowl. With mixer at low speed, beat until smooth, but not melted. Immediately pour into 4-cup mold or freezer container. Cover; freeze until firm. Unmold or remove 15 minutes before serving. Makes about 4 cups.

Honeydew, Watermelon, Peach or Pineapple Sherbet: Follow recipe for Frosty Cantaloupe Sherbet. Substitute 3 cups honeydew, watermelon, peaches or pineapple for cantaloupe.

Blueberry or Strawberry Sherbet: Follow recipe for Frosty Cantaloupe Sherbet. Substitute 3 cups whole blueberries or strawberries for cantaloupe. Makes about 3 1/2 cups.

Banana Sherbet: Follow recipe for Frosty Cantaloupe Sherbet. Increase milk to 1 1/2 cups. Substitute 2 cups sliced banana and 1 tablespoon lemon juice for cantaloupe.

EASY FROZEN YOGURT

2 containers (8 oz each) vanilla or lemon yogurt	1/4 cup Karo light corn syrup
	2 tablespoons sugar

In bowl stir together yogurt, corn syrup and sugar. Pour into 9 x 5 x 3-inch loaf pan. Freeze until firm. Turn into blender container; cover. Blend at medium speed 1 minute or until liquified. Return to loaf pan. Cover; freeze until firm. Remove 10 minutes before serving. Makes about 1 pint.

Mocha Frozen Yogurt: Follow recipe for Easy Frozen Yogurt. Substitute 2 containers (8 oz each) coffee yogurt for vanilla yogurt. Add 1 tablespoon unsweetened cocoa.

Mocha Yogurt Parfait: Follow recipe for Mocha Frozen Yogurt. After blending place 1/4 cup yogurt in each of 4 parfait glasses. Sprinkle each with 1 tablespoon chocolate wafer crumbs. Top each with another 1/4 cup yogurt. Sprinkle each with additional chocolate wafer crumbs. Freeze.

Tip: To turn frozen yogurt into a refreshing midday meal, serve it with fresh fruit and top with Strawberry Sauce.

CAKES, COOKIES AND CANDIES

Whenever and wherever good times are celebrated, cakes, cookies and candies are there. They add to the festivities and please the soul. They make waiting for them fun, a happy end to the meal, a highlight of the party, a bit of pampering to warm the day. Cakes and their frostings, cookies and candies are natural Karo creations. Karo contributes to their texture and enhances their flavor.

SPONGE CAKE

1 1/4 cups sifted cake flour	3/4 cup Karo light or dark corn syrup
1/2 cup sugar	
1/4 teaspoon salt	1/2 teaspoon vanilla
5 eggs, separated	1/2 teaspoon lemon extract
1 teaspoon cream of tartar	

Sift together flour, 1/4 cup of the sugar and salt. In large bowl with mixer at high speed beat egg whites and cream of tartar until soft peaks form. Gradually beat in remaining sugar. Slowly add corn syrup and continue beating until stiff peaks form. In small bowl with mixer at high speed beat egg yolks until thick and light in color. Beat in vanilla and lemon extract. Fold egg yolks into egg white mixture. Gradually fold in flour mixture sifting about 1/4 cup at a time over surface. Turn into ungreased 10 x 4-inch tube pan. Cut through batter with spatula to remove large bubbles. Bake in 325°F oven 50 to 55 minutes or until cake tester inserted in center comes out clean. Invert pan and cool. Loosen sides with spatula before removing from pan. Makes 12 servings.

Top to bottom: *Bourbon Cake* p. 79,
Petite Cakes p. 78, *Raisin-Spice Cake* p. 82.

NO-BAKE HOLIDAY CAKE

3 cups graham cracker crumbs
1 tablespoon grated lemon rind
1/2 teaspoon ground cinnamon
1/8 teaspoon ground allspice
1/8 teaspoon ground ginger
1 pound chopped mixed candied fruit

1 can (3 1/2 oz) flaked coconut
1 cup chopped pecans
1 cup golden raisins
1/2 cup Karo light corn syrup
1/4 cup brandy
2 tablespoons lemon juice

Line 8 1/2 x 4 1/2 x 2 1/2-inch loaf pan with foil. In large bowl stir together crumbs, lemon rind, cinnamon, allspice and ginger. Stir in candied fruit, coconut, nuts and raisins until thoroughly blended. In small bowl stir together corn syrup, brandy and lemon juice. Add to crumb mixture and mix well. Press firmly into prepared pan. Cover tightly with foil. Refrigerate at least 4 days. Turn out of pan; remove foil. Cut into thin slices with sharp knife. Makes 1 (3 lb) loaf.

PETITE CAKES

1 loaf (16 oz) frozen pound cake, thawed
1 package (16 oz) confectioners sugar
1/3 cup water
1/4 cup Karo light corn syrup

2 tablespoons corn oil
1 teaspoon vanilla
3 tubes (3/4 oz each) decorator gel

Cut cake crosswise into 8 slices. Cut each slice in half to make 16 pieces; place on wire rack over waxed paper. In small bowl with mixer at low speed beat sugar, water, corn syrup, corn oil and vanilla until smooth. Spoon icing evenly over cake pieces (icing which drips off may be reused). Let stand at room temperature about 2 hours or until set. Decorate as desired with decorator gel. Makes 16 cakes.

BOURBON CAKE

1 package (18 1/2 oz) yellow cake mix	4 eggs
1/2 cup corn starch	1/2 cup corn oil
1/2 cup sugar	1 teaspoon vanilla
1 cup water	Bourbon Glaze (recipe follows)

Grease 12-cup fluted or 10 x 4-inch tube pan. In large bowl stir together cake mix, corn starch and sugar. With mixer at low speed, beat in water, eggs, corn oil and vanilla until smooth. Increase speed to medium; beat 3 minutes. Pour into prepared pan. Bake in 350°F oven 50 to 60 minutes or until cake tester inserted in center comes out clean. Prepare Bourbon Glaze. Cool cake 15 minutes in pan. Remove; place on wire rack. While cake is still warm, pierce thoroughly with fork. Brush with 1/2 of the glaze. Let stand 1 hour. Pierce cake again; brush with remaining glaze. Store tightly covered. Makes 12 servings.

Bourbon Glaze: In 1-quart saucepan stir together 1 cup Karo light corn syrup, 1/4 cup sugar and 1/4 cup margarine. Stirring constantly, cook over medium heat until sugar is dissolved. Remove from heat; stir in 1/2 cup bourbon or orange juice. Makes 1 3/4 cups.

EASY STICKY BUNS

2 tablespoons margarine	1/4 cup raisins

1/4 cup firmly packed
    brown sugar
	1/4 teaspoon ground
	    cinnamon

1/4 cup Karo light or dark
    corn syrup
	1 can refrigerator
	    biscuits (10)

1/4 cup chopped nuts	

In 9 x 1 1/2-inch round baking pan melt margarine in 400°F oven. Remove from oven; stir in sugar, corn syrup, nuts, raisins and cinnamon. Place biscuits on top. Bake according to package directions or in 400°F oven 15 minutes or until biscuits are well browned. Let stand 5 minutes in pan; invert on serving dish. Makes 10 buns.

BRANDIED FRUIT CAKE

2 pounds mixed candied fruit	1/2 teaspoon ground nutmeg
1 pound raisins	1/2 cup margarine
1 cup chopped dates	1 cup sugar
1 1/2 cups chopped nuts	1 cup Karo dark corn syrup
4 1/4 cups unsifted flour	3 eggs
1/2 teaspoon baking soda	1/2 cup brandy
1/2 teaspoon ground cinnamon	1/2 teaspoon vanilla
1/2 teaspoon ground allspice	1/2 cup Karo light corn syrup
1/2 teaspoon ground cloves	

Grease 10 x 4-inch tube pan. Line bottom with brown paper. In bowl stir together candied fruit, raisins, dates and nuts. Stir in 1/4 cup of the flour; set aside. In medium bowl stir together remaining 4 cups flour, baking soda, cinnamon, allspice, cloves and nutmeg; set aside. In large bowl stir margarine to soften. Add sugar and dark corn syrup; mix well. Beat in eggs, one at a time. Stir in brandy and vanilla. Gradually stir in flour mixture until well blended. Stir in fruit mixture. Turn into prepared pan; cover tightly with foil. Bake in 300°F oven 3 hours or until cake tester inserted in center comes out clean. Cool completely. Remove from pan. Peel off paper. Wrap in plastic wrap, then foil. Store in tightly covered container at least 1 month. Glaze a day or two before serving. To glaze, bring light corn syrup to boil. Brush over top and sides of cake. Decorate as desired with candied fruit. Makes 1 (6 lb) cake.

Tip: To follow traditional fruit cake storage, wrap the fruit cake in a brandy-soaked cheesecloth, then, adding a few pieces of raw, unpeeled apple, seal it in a cake tin. As the cheesecloth dries out, soak it in additional brandy.

Top to bottom: *Brownies* p. 87,
Nut Filled Pastries p. 89,
Swedish Jam Cookies p. 91,
Alphabet Cookies p. 89,
Ginger Almond Treats p. 90.

RAISIN-SPICE CAKE

1 package (12 oz) pitted prunes	1 teaspoon ground cinnamon
1 package (8 oz) pitted dates	1 teaspoon ground nutmeg
3 cups raisins	1/2 cup margarine
1 cup dry white wine	1/2 cup sugar
1 cup rum	1/2 cup Karo light corn syrup
2 1/2 cups unsifted flour	3 eggs
1 teaspoon baking powder	1 teaspoon vanilla

Into medium bowl snip prunes and dates. Stir in raisins, wine and rum; cover. Let stand in cool place, stirring occasionally, 3 days. Grease and flour 2 (9 x 5 x 3-inch) loaf pans. In small bowl stir together flour, baking powder, cinnamon and nutmeg. In large bowl with mixer at medium speed beat margarine, sugar and corn syrup until well blended. Add eggs; beat until smooth. Add flour mixture; beat just until moistened. Stir in fruit mixture and vanilla. Turn into prepared pans. Bake in 300°F oven 1 hour 25 minutes or until cake tester inserted in center comes out clean. Cool in pan 30 minutes. Remove and cool on wire racks. Makes 2 loaves.

MINCEMEAT BANANA BREAD

1 package (9 oz) condensed mincemeat	1/2 cup Karo dark corn syrup
1/4 cup brandy	1/2 cup milk
3 cups unsifted flour	1/4 cup sugar
1 tablespoon baking powder	1/4 cup corn oil
1 teaspoon salt	1 egg
1 cup mashed ripe banana	

Grease and flour 9 x 5 x 3-inch loaf pan. In small bowl break up mincemeat; add brandy and soak until soft. Stir together flour, baking powder and salt. In large bowl beat together banana, corn syrup, milk, sugar, corn oil and egg. Beat in mincemeat. Mix in flour mixture. Turn into prepared pan.

Bake in 350°F oven 1 1/2 hours or until cake tester inserted in center comes out clean. Cool on wire rack 5 minutes; remove from pan. Cool completely. Makes 1 loaf.

APPLE UPSIDE DOWN CAKE

2 medium apples, peeled, cored	1/2 cup chopped walnuts
2 tablespoons margarine	2 1/4 cups buttermilk baking mix
1/3 cup Karo light or dark corn syrup	1/4 cup sugar
2 tablespoons brown sugar	1/2 teaspoon ground allspice
1 teaspoon ground cinnamon	1 egg
	3/4 cup milk

Cut apples crosswise into 9 slices. In saucepan melt margarine over medium heat. In 8 x 8 x 2-inch baking dish mix together margarine, corn syrup, brown sugar and cinnamon. Arrange apple slices in bottom of dish. Sprinkle with nuts. Bake in 350°F oven 15 minutes. In large bowl stir together baking mix, sugar and allspice. Beat together egg and milk. Add to dry mixture and stir until moistened. Pour over hot apple slices. Bake in 350°F oven 35 minutes or until cake tester inserted in center comes out clean. Loosen edges; invert on serving platter and cool 10 minutes before removing from baking dish. Serve warm. Makes 9 servings.

Tip: For a nearly perfect combination, serve warm Apple Upside Down Cake with cool and creamy ice cream.

MINI FRUIT CAKES

2 pounds mixed candied fruit, finely chopped	1/2 teaspoon salt
1 pound pitted dates, finely chopped	4 eggs
1 pound finely chopped pecans	1/4 cup firmly packed brown sugar
2 cups unsifted flour	1/2 cup Karo dark corn syrup
2 teaspoons baking powder	1/4 cup corn oil

Grease and flour 36 (2 1/2 x 1 3/4-inch) muffin cups. In large bowl stir together fruit, dates and nuts; set aside. In small bowl stir together flour, baking powder and salt. In large bowl with mixer at medium speed beat eggs until foamy. Add brown sugar, corn syrup and corn oil; beat until thoroughly mixed. Gradually add flour mixture; beat until smooth. Pour batter over fruit mixture. Mix until fruit is thoroughly coated. Spoon into prepared muffin cups filling almost full. Bake in 275°F oven 1 hour or until cake tester inserted in center comes out clean. Cool in pan 10 minutes. Remove and cool on wire rack. Wrap each cake tightly in plastic wrap. Store tightly covered at room temperature, or for easier slicing store in refrigerator. Makes 36 cakes.

Tip: There is nothing more appreciated than the holiday gift of superb home-baked treats such as these miniature cakes. Wrap each individually in plastic wrap and tie with a bright plain ribbon.

84

FLUFFY FROSTING

2 egg whites, at room
   temperature
1/4 teaspoon cream of
   tartar
1/4 teaspoon salt

1/4 cup sugar
3/4 cup Karo light
   corn syrup
1 1/4 teaspoons vanilla

In small bowl with mixer at high speed beat egg whites, cream of tartar and salt until soft peaks form. Gradually beat in sugar until smooth and glossy. Gradually beat in corn syrup and vanilla until stiff peaks form. If desired, beat in food color. Makes enough frosting for 9-inch layer cake or 1 (13 x 9 x 2-inch) cake.

Orange Frosting: Follow recipe for Fluffy Frosting. Use 1 tablespoon grated orange rind and 1/2 teaspoon orange extract. Omit vanilla.

Lemon Frosting: Follow recipe for Fluffy Frosting. Use 2 teaspoons grated lemon rind. Omit vanilla.

Coconut Frosting: Prepare Fluffy Frosting. Fold in 1 cup flaked coconut.

Coffee Frosting: Follow recipe for Fluffy Frosting. Add 1 tablespoon instant coffee powder, crushed, with corn syrup.

Spice Frosting: Follow recipe for Fluffy Frosting. Substitute Karo dark corn syrup for light corn syrup. Add 1/2 teaspoon ground ginger, 1/4 teaspoon ground cinnamon and dash ground cloves with corn syrup. Omit vanilla.

Chocolate Marble Frosting: Prepare Fluffy Frosting. Swirl 1 package (1 oz) no-melt unsweetened chocolate into frosting, cutting in with spatula to give marbled effect.

Tutti-Frutti Frosting: Prepare Fluffy Frosting. Fold in 1/4 cup chopped nuts, 1/4 cup raisins and 1/4 cup chopped candied cherries.

RICH CHOCOLATE FROSTING

2 packages (3 oz each) cream cheese	1 package (16 oz) confectioners sugar
1/2 teaspoon vanilla	4 squares (1 oz each)
1/8 teaspoon salt	unsweetened choco-
1/2 cup Karo light corn syrup	late, melted, cooled
	1 to 2 tablespoons water

In large bowl with mixer at medium speed beat cream cheese, vanilla and salt until smooth. Slowly pour in corn syrup while beating; beat until well blended. Gradually add confectioners sugar, beating well after each addition. Add chocolate; beat until smooth. If too thick, beat in water 1 teaspoon at a time to obtain desired consistency. Makes enough frosting for 9-inch layer cake.

Mocha Frosting: Follow recipe for Rich Chocolate Frosting. Add 3 tablespoons crushed instant coffee powder (not freeze dried) to mixture after blending in corn syrup. Reduce chocolate to 3 squares.

Orange-Chocolate Frosting: Follow recipe for Rich Chocolate Frosting. Add 1 1/2 tablespoons grated orange rind to mixture after blending in corn syrup. Reduce chocolate to 3 squares.

CREAMY LEMON FROSTING

1 cup margarine	1 tablespoon lemon juice
2/3 cup Karo light corn syrup	Food color
5 1/2 cups confectioners sugar	

In large bowl with mixer at medium speed beat margarine and corn syrup until blended. With wooden spoon gradually beat in confectioners sugar and lemon juice until smooth. Tint with food color. Makes enough frosting for 9-inch layer cake.

BROWNIES

1/2 cup margarine	2 squares (1 oz each) unsweetened chocolate, melted
1/2 cup sugar	
1/2 teaspoon vanilla	
1/2 cup Karo dark corn syrup	1/2 cup unsifted flour
	1/2 teaspoon salt
2 eggs, unbeaten	1/2 cup chopped walnuts

Grease 9 x 9 x 2-inch baking pan. In small bowl stir margarine to soften. Stir in sugar and vanilla. Add corn syrup and beat well. Beat in eggs. Stir in chocolate, flour and salt. Fold in nuts. Turn into prepared pan. Bake in 325°F oven 35 to 40 minutes or until cake tester inserted in center comes out clean. Cut into squares while warm. Cool. Makes 16.

MARBLED BROWNIES

1/3 cup margarine	1/2 teaspoon salt
1/3 cup sugar	2 squares (1 oz each) semisweet chocolate, melted
1/3 cup Karo light corn syrup	
1 egg	1 package (3 oz) cream cheese
1 cup unsifted flour	
1/2 teaspoon baking powder	

Grease 9 x 9 x 2-inch baking pan. In large bowl with mixer at medium speed beat margarine and sugar until well mixed. Beat in corn syrup and egg. Stir together flour, baking powder and salt. At low speed beat flour mixture into margarine mixture until combined. Stir 1/2 cup of batter into melted chocolate. Add cream cheese to batter remaining in bowl; beat until smooth. Turn cream cheese mixture into prepared pan. With metal spatula swirl chocolate mixture through cream cheese mixture. Bake in 350°F oven 40 minutes. Cool. Cut into bars. Makes 16.

LINZER BARS

1 3/4 cups unsifted flour
1/4 cup sugar
1/4 cup firmly packed
    brown sugar
1/2 teaspoon baking
    powder
1/2 teaspoon salt
1/2 teaspoon ground
    cinnamon

1/2 cup margarine
1/4 cup Karo dark corn
    syrup
1 egg, slightly beaten
1/2 cup raspberry jam
2 tablespoons flour

In large bowl stir together 1 3/4 cups flour, sugar, brown sugar, baking powder, salt and cinnamon. With pastry blender or two knives cut in margarine until coarse crumbs form. With fork stir in corn syrup and egg just until mixed. Reserve 1/2 cup batter. Press remaining batter into ungreased 9 x 9 x 2-inch baking pan. Spread with jam. Stir 2 tablespoons flour into the reserved batter. On floured surface roll out to 1/4-inch thickness. Cut into 1/4-inch wide strips. Lattice strips over jam. Bake in 375°F oven 30 minutes or until set. Cool. Cut into bars. Makes 36.

CHEWY-NUT SQUARES

1 1/4 cups unsifted flour
1 cup firmly packed
    brown sugar
1/2 cup margarine
2 eggs, slightly beaten
1/2 cup Karo dark corn
    syrup

1 teaspoon vanilla
1/4 teaspoon salt
1 cup chopped pecans
1/2 cup flaked coconut

In small bowl mix together 1 cup of the flour and 1/2 cup of the sugar. With pastry blender or two knives cut in margarine until fine crumbs form. Pat into 8 x 8 x 2-inch baking pan. Bake in 350°F oven 20 minutes; remove. In medium bowl stir together remaining flour and sugar. Add eggs, corn syrup, vanilla and salt. Beat until smooth. Stir in nuts and coconut. Spread over crust. Bake 30 minutes or until top is set. Cool. Cut into 2-inch squares. Makes 16.

NUT FILLED PASTRIES

2 1/2 cups unsifted flour
1 cup margarine
2 egg yolks, slightly beaten
1/2 cup dairy sour cream

2 cups ground pecans or walnuts
2/3 cup Karo dark corn syrup
Confectioners sugar

Place flour in large bowl. With pastry blender or two knives cut in margarine until coarse crumbs form. Stir in egg yolks and sour cream until well mixed. Turn onto floured surface; knead until smooth. Cover; chill 20 minutes. In small bowl stir together nuts and corn syrup. On lightly floured surface roll out 1/2 of dough at a time to 1/8-inch thickness. Keep remaining dough refrigerated. Cut dough into 2-inch squares. Put 1/2 teaspoon nut filling diagonally across square. Moisten 2 opposite corners slightly with water. Fold over filling overlapping slightly. Place on cookie sheet. Bake in 400°F oven 12 minutes or until edges are lightly browned. Cool. Sprinkle with confectioners sugar. Makes about 8 dozen.

ALPHABET COOKIES

1 cup margarine
1/4 cup creamy peanut butter
1/2 cup Karo light corn syrup

1/2 cup sugar
1 teaspoon vanilla
3 cups unsifted flour

In large bowl with mixer at medium speed beat margarine, peanut butter, corn syrup, sugar and vanilla until well mixed. At low speed gradually add flour, beating until well blended. Cover; chill 1 hour. To form initials, roll dough into 1 1/2-inch balls; then roll on smooth surface into a rope 8-inches long. Shape rope into desired letter directly on cookie sheet. Keep remaining dough refrigerated while working. Bake in 350°F oven 12 to 15 minutes or until lightly browned. Cool on wire rack. Makes 1 Alphabet (26 cookies).

89

FINNISH CARDAMOM COOKIES

2 cups unsifted flour
1/2 cup sugar
1/2 teaspoon baking soda
1/2 cup Karo dark corn
    syrup
1/2 cup margarine
2 teaspoons grated
    orange rind

1 teaspoon ground
    cardamom
1/4 teaspoon ground
    ginger
1/4 teaspoon ground
    cloves
1 egg

In bowl stir together flour, sugar and baking soda. In 1-quart saucepan mix together corn syrup, margarine, orange rind, cardamom, ginger and cloves. Stirring constantly, cook over medium heat until margarine is melted and mixture boils. Remove from heat. In large bowl beat egg until thick and lemon colored. Slowly stir in syrup mixture. Add flour mixture all at once; mix until well blended. Drop 2 inches apart by teaspoonfuls onto well greased cookie sheet. Bake in 350°F oven 8 to 10 minutes or until lightly browned. Immediately remove from cookie sheet. Cool on wire rack. Makes about 4 1/2 dozen.

GINGER ALMOND TREATS

2 1/4 cups unsifted flour
1 1/2 teaspoons baking soda
1/2 teaspoon salt
3/4 cup margarine
1 cup firmly packed
    brown sugar
1 egg

1/4 cup Karo dark corn
    syrup
1 tablespoon grated
    ginger root
    Whole blanched
    almonds

Stir together flour, baking soda and salt. In large bowl with mixer at medium speed beat margarine and sugar until smooth. Add egg, corn syrup and ginger root; beat until well mixed. Add flour mixture stirring just until mixed. Drop 2 inches apart by heaping teaspoonfuls onto ungreased cookie sheet. Press an almond into center of each. Bake in 350°F oven 10 to 12 minutes or until lightly browned. (Do not overbake as cookies harden upon cooling.) Cool on wire rack. Makes 4 dozen.

SPICE SNAPS

3 1/2 cups sifted flour
2 teaspoons ground ginger
1 teaspoon ground cardamom
1 teaspoon ground cinnamon
1/2 teaspoon ground cloves
1 teaspoon salt
1/4 teaspoon baking soda
3/4 cup margarine
1/2 cup sugar
1 egg
1/2 cup Karo dark corn syrup
2 tablespoons grated lemon rind
2 tablespoons brandy or lemon juice

Sift together flour, ginger, cardamom, cinnamon, cloves, salt and baking soda. In large bowl with mixer at medium speed beat margarine and sugar until blended. Add egg, corn syrup, lemon rind and brandy; beat until creamy. Gradually add flour mixture; beat just until blended. Cover; chill several hours or overnight. On lightly floured surface roll out 1/4 of dough at a time to 1/16-inch thickness; keep remaining dough refrigerated. Cut with 2-inch round cutter or glass. Place on lightly greased cookie sheet. Bake in 350°F oven 6 minutes or until very lightly browned around edge. Cool on wire rack. Makes about 7 dozen.

SWEDISH JAM COOKIES

1 cup margarine
1/2 cup sugar
1/2 cup Karo dark corn syrup
2 eggs, separated
2 1/2 cups unsifted flour
2 cups finely chopped walnuts
Tart jam or jelly

In large bowl with mixer at medium speed beat margarine and sugar until smooth. Beat in corn syrup and egg yolks until well mixed. Stir in flour until well blended. Chill dough 20 to 25 minutes or until firm enough to handle. Shape into 1-inch balls. Dip into slightly beaten egg white. Roll in nuts. Place 2 inches apart on greased cookie sheet. With thumb make indentation in center of each cookie. Bake in 325°F oven 20 minutes or until golden. Remove from oven. While still warm fill with a small amount of jam. Cool on wire rack. Makes about 4 dozen.

91

OLD FASHIONED HARD CANDY

2 cups firmly packed light brown sugar	1/2 cup margarine
1/4 cup Karo dark corn syrup	2 tablespoons white vinegar
	2 tablespoons water

In medium saucepan stir together sugar, corn syrup, margarine, vinegar and water. Stirring constantly, cook over medium heat until mixture boils. Continue cooking, stirring occasionally, until temperature reaches 300°F on candy thermometer or until small amount of mixture when dropped into very cold water, separates into threads which are hard and brittle. Drop mixture by teaspoonfuls onto greased cookie sheets. Cool. Store in tightly covered container. Makes about 1 pound.

LOLLIPOPS

2 cups sugar	1 1/2 teaspoons peppermint, spearmint, lemon or orange extract
1 cup Karo light corn syrup	
1/2 cup water	Food color

Place 42 lollipop sticks, 4 inches apart on greased baking sheets or foil. In heavy 2-quart saucepan stir together sugar, corn syrup and water. Stirring constantly, cook over medium heat until mixture boils. Continue cooking, without stirring, until temperature reaches 300°F on candy thermometer or until small amount of mixture dropped into very cold water separates into threads which are hard and brittle. Cool slightly. Stir in flavor and food color just enough to mix. Drop candy mixture from tip of teaspoon over one end of each stick to form 2-inch circle. (If mixture hardens before all lollipops are made stir over low heat just until mixture is melted.) Makes 42.

Hard Candy Drops: Follow recipe for Lollipop mixture; cool slightly. Stir in extract and food color just enough to mix. Or for a variety of colors and flavors, divide candy mixture into 3 small, hot, dry saucepans. Separately, color and flavor with 1/4 teaspoon desired extract. Drop candy mixture by teaspoonfuls onto cookie sheets or foil.

CHOCOLATE CARAMELS

1 1/4 cups sugar
1/2 cup Karo light corn
  syrup
1/2 cup Karo dark corn
  syrup

1 cup heavy cream
1 tablespoon margarine
2 squares (1 oz each)
  unsweetened
  chocolate

Grease 9 x 9 x 2-inch baking pan. In heavy 3-quart saucepan stir together sugar, corn syrups and cream. Stirring constantly, cook over medium heat until mixture boils and sugar is dissolved. Continue cooking, stirring occasionally, until temperature reaches 250°F on candy thermometer or until small amount of mixture dropped into very cold water forms a ball which is hard enough to hold its shape, yet plastic. Remove from heat; stir in margarine and chocolate until blended. Pour into prepared pan. Cool 1 hour. Cut into 1-inch squares. Makes 81.

Vanilla Caramels: Follow recipe of Chocolate Caramels. Use 1 cup light corn syrup, 2 tablespoons margarine and 1 teaspoon vanilla. Omit dark corn syrup and chocolate. Makes 81.

MAPLE-WALNUT CARAMELS

1 cup Karo light or dark
  corn syrup
1 cup light cream
1 cup sugar

1/4 cup margarine
1 cup coarsely chopped
  walnuts
1 1/2 teaspoons maple flavor

Grease 8 x 8 x 2-inch baking pan. In heavy 3-quart saucepan stir together corn syrup, cream, sugar and margarine. Stirring constantly, cook over medium heat until mixture boils and sugar is dissolved. Continue cooking, stirring occasionally, until temperature reaches 242°F on candy thermometer or until small amount of mixture dropped into very cold water forms a ball which is hard enough to hold its shape, yet plastic. Remove from heat; stir in nuts and maple flavor. Pour into prepared pan. Cool 1 hour. Cut into 1-inch squares. Makes 64.

93

THIN TOFFEE CRUNCH

1 3/4 cups sugar	3/4 cup margarine
1/3 cup Karo light corn syrup	Chocolate Glaze (recipe follows)
1/4 cup heavy cream	

Line 2 cookie sheets with foil; grease. In heavy 2-quart saucepan stir together sugar, corn syrup and cream until well blended. Stirring constantly, cook over low heat until mixture boils. Add margarine. Continue cooking, stirring occasionally, until temperature reaches 285°F on candy thermometer or until small amount of mixture dropped into very cold water separates into threads which are hard but not brittle. Pour onto prepared cookie sheets; spread with greased spatula to cover entire surface. Cool. Spread with Chocolate Glaze. Chill 1 hour. Break into pieces. Store in cool place. Makes about 1 1/4 pounds.

Chocolate Glaze: In small saucepan over very low heat melt 2 squares (1 oz each) semisweet chocolate, 2 squares (1 oz each) unsweetened chocolate and 1/4 cup margarine with 1 tablespoon Karo light corn syrup. Stir until smooth. Remove from heat; beat until cool but still pourable.

TOASTED ALMOND BRITTLE

1 cup Karo light or dark corn syrup	1 teaspoon baking soda
1 cup sugar	1 teaspoon vanilla
1/4 cup water	1/4 teaspoon almond extract
2 tablespoons margarine	
1 1/2 cups slivered almonds, toasted	

Grease 2 cookie sheets. In heavy 3-quart saucepan stir together corn syrup, sugar, water and margarine. Stirring constantly, cook over medium heat until mixture boils and sugar is dissolved. Continue cooking, without stirring, until temperature reaches 280°F on candy thermometer or until small amount of mixture dropped into very cold water separates into threads which are hard but not brittle. Gradually stir in nuts. Stirring frequently, cook until temperature reaches 300°F on candy thermometer or until small amount of mixture dropped into very cold water separates into threads which are hard and brittle. Remove from heat; stir in baking soda, vanilla and almond extract. Immediately pour onto cookie sheets. Spread evenly to edges with greased metal spatula. Cool. Break into pieces. Store in tightly covered container. Makes about 1 1/4 pounds.

CANDY APPLES

8 medium red apples	1/2 cup water
8 flat wooden skewers or spoons	1/4 cup red cinnamon candies
2 cups sugar	10 drops red food color
1 cup Karo light corn syrup	

Wash and dry apples; remove stems and insert skewers into stem ends. In heavy 2-quart saucepan stir together sugar, corn syrup and water. Stirring constantly, cook over medium heat until mixture boils and sugar is dissolved. Continue cooking, without stirring, until temperature reaches 250°F on candy thermometer or until small amount of mixture dropped into very cold water forms a ball which is hard enough to hold its shape, yet plastic. Add cinnamon candies and continue cooking until temperature reaches 285°F on candy thermometer or until small amount of mixture dropped into very cold water separates into threads which are hard, but not brittle. Remove from heat. Stir in food color. Hold each apple by its skewer and quickly twirl in syrup, tilting pan to cover apple. Remove from syrup; allow excess to drip off, then twirl to spread syrup smoothly over apple. If desired, roll bottom quarter of apple in slightly crushed corn flakes or shredded coconut. Place on lightly greased cookie sheet to cool. (If mixture hardens before all apples are dipped, stir over low heat just until mixture is melted.) Store in cool place. Makes 8.

TOASTED ALMOND NOUGAT

2 cups Karo light corn syrup	2 cups whole un-blanched toasted almonds
2 cups sugar	
1/4 cup water	3 tablespoons margarine
1/4 teaspoon salt	1 1/2 teaspoons vanilla
2 egg whites	

Grease 13 x 9 x 2-inch baking pan. In heavy 3-quart sauce-pan stir together corn syrup, sugar, water and salt. Stirring constantly, cook over medium heat until mixture boils. Continue cooking without stirring until temperature reaches 250°F on candy thermometer or until small amount of mixture dropped into very cold water forms a ball which is hard enough to hold its shape, yet plastic. Just before syrup reaches 250°F, in large bowl with mixer at high speed beat egg whites until stiff peaks form. With mixer at high speed slowly pour 1/4 (about 1 cup) of the syrup over egg whites. Continue beating 5 minutes or until stiff peaks form. Cook remaining syrup over low heat, without stirring, until temperature reaches 280°F on candy thermometer or until small amount of mixture dropped into very cold water separates into threads which are hard but not brittle. Gradually stir in nuts to prevent syrup from cooling. Continue cooking until temperature reaches 300°F on candy thermometer or until small amount of mixture dropped into very cold water separates into threads which are hard and brittle. Stir in margarine and vanilla. While beating with wooden spoon, slowly add remaining syrup to egg white mixture. Spread nougat in prepared pan. Let stand overnight in cool place before cutting. Cut into 1 x 1 1/2-inch rectangles. Wrap individually. Store in tightly covered container. Makes 2 1/2 pounds.

Top to bottom: *Old-Fashioned Popcorn Balls* p. 101, *Brown Sugar Divinity* p. 98, *Chocolate Fudge* p. 102, *Spirited Fruit Balls* p. 99, *No-Cook Fondant* p. 104, *Chocolate Dipped Strawberries* p. 103.

COFFEE LIQUEUR CANDY

2/3 cup strong coffee	2 cups sugar
1 tablespoon white vinegar	2/3 cup Karo light corn syrup
2 tablespoons coffee liqueur	1/2 cup heavy cream
	1/8 teaspoon salt

Grease 8 x 8 x 2-inch baking pan. In small saucepan stir together coffee and vinegar. Cook over medium heat until liquid is reduced to 2 tablespoons. Remove from heat; add liqueur. In heavy 2-quart saucepan, stir together sugar, corn syrup, cream and salt. Stirring constantly, cook over low heat until mixture boils. Cover and boil 3 minutes. Uncover and continue cooking, without stirring, until temperature reaches 260°F on candy thermometer or until small amount of mixture dropped into very cold water forms a ball which is hard enough to hold its shape, yet plastic. Continue cooking, stirring constantly, until temperature reaches 300°F on candy thermometer or until small amount of mixture dropped into very cold water separates into threads which are hard and brittle. Remove from heat. Stir in coffee mixture. Pour into prepared pan. Cool 5 minutes or until film forms on top. Beginning at edge use a sharp knife to mark the candy into 1/2-inch squares. (Do not break through film.) Using flat metal spatula continue pressing along marks, pressing deeper each time. When spatula may be pressed to bottom of pan, candy will be shaped in puffs. Cool completely. Turn out on board and break into pieces. Makes about 1 1/4 pounds.

BROWN SUGAR DIVINITY

1 cup firmly packed light brown sugar	Dash salt
1 cup sugar	2 egg whites
2/3 cup water	1 teaspoon vanilla
1/3 cup Karo light corn syrup	1 cup chopped nuts

In heavy 2-quart saucepan stir together brown sugar, sugar, water, corn syrup and salt. Stirring constantly, cook over medium heat until mixture boils. Reduce heat; continue to boil gently, without stirring, until temperature reaches 262°F on candy thermometer or until small amount of mixture dropped into very cold water forms a ball which is hard enough to hold its shape, yet plastic. Just before temperature reaches 262°F, in large bowl with mixer at high speed beat egg whites until soft peaks form. Beating constantly at high speed, pour hot syrup in fine stream over egg whites. Beat in vanilla. Continue beating until mixture begins to lose its gloss. Stir in nuts. Drop by teaspoonfuls onto waxed paper. Makes about 1 pound.

Divinity Squares: Follow recipe for Brown Sugar Divinity. Spread in lightly greased 8 x 8 x 2-inch pan. Let set. Cut into squares. Makes 64.

SPIRITED FRUIT BALLS

1 cup finely chopped candied pineapple	1/4 cup margarine
1 cup finely chopped dried peaches or apricots	1/4 cup nonfat dry milk powder
1 cup finely chopped macadamia nuts	1/4 cup Karo light corn syrup
1 tablespoon grated orange rind	3 cups graham cracker crumbs
1/2 cup orange-flavored liqueur	1/2 cup confectioners sugar

In small bowl stir together pineapple, peaches, nuts, orange rind and liqueur. Let stand at least 1 hour. In large bowl with mixer at medium speed beat margarine until smooth. Add milk powder and corn syrup, mixing until blended. At low speed gradually add cracker crumbs. Mix until coarse crumbs form. Add fruit mixture; mix well. Shape into balls using 1 tablespoon mixture for each. Roll in sugar. Store in tightly covered container at least 1 week to blend flavors. Makes 55.

SPICED SUGARED NUTS

1 cup sugar	1/4 teaspoon ground allspice
1/3 cup water	1/4 teaspoon salt
1/4 cup Karo light corn syrup	2 cups walnut or pecan halves
1 teaspoon ground cinnamon	1 teaspoon vanilla

Grease 15 1/2 x 10 1/2 x 1-inch jelly roll pan. In heavy 2-quart saucepan stir together sugar, water, corn syrup, cinnamon, allspice and salt. Stirring constantly, cook over medium heat until mixture boils. Continue cooking, stirring occasionally, until temperature reaches 235°F on candy thermometer or until small amount of mixture dropped into very cold water forms a soft ball which flattens on removal from water. Remove from heat. Add nuts and vanilla. Stir until mixture begins to thicken and get lighter in color. Pour onto prepared pan. Working quickly with two forks separate nuts into individual pieces. Cool. Store in tightly covered container. Makes about 1 pound.

Candied Walnuts: Follow recipe for Spiced Sugared Nuts. Omit cinnamon, allspice and vanilla. Use 2 cups walnut halves and add 1 teaspoon rum extract with walnuts.

HOLIDAY RUM BALLS

3 1/2 cups vanilla wafer crumbs (about 12 oz)	1/4 cup unsweetened cocoa
1 1/2 cups confectioners sugar	1/3 cup light or dark rum
1 cup finely chopped pecans	1/3 cup Karo light corn syrup

In large bowl stir together crumbs, 1 cup of the confectioners sugar, nuts and cocoa. Stir in rum and corn syrup until well blended. Shape into 1-inch balls. Roll in remaining confectioners sugar. Store in tightly covered container. Makes about 4 1/2 dozen.

NO-COOK ORANGE BALLS

1/4 cup Karo light corn syrup	1 package (12 oz) vanilla wafers, crushed
3 tablespoons orange marmalade	Confectioners sugar
2 tablespoons orange-flavored liqueur	

In bowl stir together corn syrup, marmalade and liqueur. Stir in crumbs until moistened. Knead with hands until well mixed. Shape into 1-inch balls. Roll in confectioners sugar. Store in tightly covered container at least 1 week to blend flavors. Makes 2 1/2 dozen.

OLD-FASHIONED POPCORN BALLS

2 quarts popped corn	1/4 cup water
1 cup Karo light or dark corn syrup	1 teaspoon white vinegar
1 cup firmly packed dark brown sugar	2 tablespoons margarine

Place popcorn in large bowl or pan. In heavy 2-quart saucepan stir together corn syrup, sugar, water and vinegar. Stirring constantly, cook over medium heat until mixture boils. Continue cooking, stirring occasionally, until temperature reaches 260°F on candy thermometer or until small amount of mixture dropped into very cold water forms a ball which is hard enough to hold its shape, yet plastic. Remove from heat; stir in margarine. Slowly pour over popcorn, stirring to coat well. When cool enough to handle, yet still quite warm, quickly shape into balls. Wrap individually in plastic wrap. Makes about 10 (3-inch) balls.

PEANUT ROLL

1 1/4 cups sugar	1 teaspoon vanilla
3/4 cup Karo light or dark corn syrup	1 cup dry roasted peanuts
1/2 cup creamy or super chunk peanut butter	1 cup whole almonds

Grease 13 x 9 x 2-inch baking pan. In 2-quart saucepan stirring frequently, bring sugar and corn syrup to boil over medium heat and boil 1 minute. Remove from heat. Stir in peanut butter and vanilla until smooth. Stir in nuts. Pour into prepared pan. Let stand until cool enough to handle. Divide in half. Shape each half into log 1 1/2 inches in diameter. Wrap in plastic wrap. Chill 3 hours or until firm. To serve, let stand at room temperature about 15 minutes; cut into 1/4-inch slices. Makes 1 3/4 pounds.

CHOCOLATE FUDGE

3 cups sugar	2 squares (1 oz each) unsweetened chocolate
3/4 cup milk	
2 tablespoons Karo light or dark corn syrup	3 tablespoons margarine
	1 teaspoon vanilla

Grease 8 x 8 x 2-inch pan. In heavy 3-quart saucepan stir together sugar, milk, corn syrup and chocolate. Stirring constantly, cook over medium heat until mixture boils. Continue cooking, stirring occasionally until temperature reaches 238°F on candy thermometer or until small amount of mixture dropped into very cold water forms a soft ball which flattens on removal from water. Remove from heat. Add margarine and vanilla. *Do not stir.* Cool to lukewarm (110°F). Beat until fudge begins to thicken and begins to lose its gloss. Quickly pour into prepared pan. Cool; cut into squares. Makes 1 1/2 pounds.

Peanut Butter Fudge: Follow recipe for Chocolate Fudge. Omit chocolate and margarine. Add 1/4 cup super chunk peanut butter with vanilla. *Do not stir.* Continue as above. Makes 1 1/2 pounds.

QUICK CHOCOLATE FUDGE

1/4 cup margarine	1 teaspoon vanilla
3 squares (1 oz each) un-sweetened chocolate	1 package (16 oz) confectioners sugar
1/2 cup Karo light corn syrup	1/2 cup chopped nuts or 1 cup miniature marshmallows
1 tablespoon water	

Grease 8 x 8 x 2-inch baking pan. In 2-quart saucepan melt margarine and chocolate over low heat. Stir in corn syrup, water and vanilla. Remove from heat. Add confectioners sugar and nuts. Stir until mixture is smooth. Turn into prepared pan. Cool. Cut into squares. Makes 1 3/4 pounds.

Quick Brown Sugar Fudge: Follow recipe for Quick Chocolate Fudge. Omit chocolate and water. Melt 1/2 cup firmly packed brown sugar with margarine. Use dark corn syrup.

CHOCOLATE DIPPED STRAWBERRIES

4 squares (1 oz each) semisweet chocolate	1/4 cup margarine
4 squares (1 oz each) un-sweetened chocolate	1/4 cup Karo light corn syrup
	Strawberries

In 1-quart saucepan heat chocolate, margarine and corn syrup over very low heat until melted; stir until smooth. Remove from heat; beat with wooden spoon until cool but still pourable. Using two forks dip fruit halfway into chocolate. Place on waxed paper. Refrigerate overnight. Store in one layer in tightly covered container in refrigerator. Makes 1 1/3 cups.

Note: Assorted dried fruits such as apricots, peaches and pears may be used in place of strawberries.

103

MARSHMALLOWS

1/4 cup corn starch
1/4 cup confectioners
    sugar
  1 envelope unflavored
    gelatin

1/3 cup cold water
1/2 cup sugar
2/3 cup Karo light corn
    syrup
1/2 teaspoon vanilla

In small bowl stir together corn starch and confectioners sugar. Grease 10 x 6 x 1 3/4-inch baking dish; dust with 2 tablespoons of the corn starch mixture. In small saucepan sprinkle gelatin over cold water; stir in sugar. Stirring constantly, bring to boil over low heat. In small bowl with mixer at high speed beat gelatin mixture and corn syrup about 15 minutes or until soft peaks form. Stir in vanilla. Turn into prepared dish; smooth top with spatula. Let stand several hours or until set. To remove from dish, loosen edges with warm dry knife; invert over board sprinkled lightly with some of the corn starch mixture. Cut into 1-inch squares using warm dry sharp knife. Roll in remaining corn starch mixture. Place on wire rack and let dry several hours before storing. Store in single layer in tightly covered container in cool dry place. Makes 3/4 pound.

NO-COOK FONDANT

1/3 cup margarine
1/3 cup Karo light corn
    syrup
  1 teaspoon vanilla
1/2 teaspoon salt

1 package (16 oz)
    confectioners sugar,
    sifted
Food color

In large bowl with mixer at medium speed beat margarine, corn syrup, vanilla and salt until smooth. Add confectioners sugar all at once. With wooden spoon, then with hands mix until smooth. Turn out onto board and knead until mixture is well blended and smooth. Tint and shape as desired. Store in cool place. Makes 1 1/3 pounds.

Patties: Follow recipe for No-Cook Fondant. Omit vanilla. Use 1 teaspoon peppermint or wintergreen flavoring, 2 teaspoons orange extract or 1 teaspoon lemon extract. Shape into balls and flatten or roll thin and cut into small rounds.

MARZIPAN

3	tablespoons Karo light corn syrup		Dash salt
1/4	teaspoon vanilla	1	tablespoon milk
1/4	teaspoon almond extract	1 1/2	cups sifted confectioners sugar
		1	cup almond paste

In bowl stir together corn syrup, vanilla, almond extract and salt. Stir in milk. Add confectioners sugar; mix well. Stir in almond paste until thoroughly mixed. Shape as desired. Let stand uncovered to dry thoroughly. Store in tightly covered container. Makes about 3/4 pound.

General Directions for Tinting: Tint marzipan by kneading in liquid or paste food colors. Use corn syrup to help stick pieces of marzipan together. To make "paint" mix small amount of paste color into light corn syrup. Apply to marzipan using thin brush.

Stuffed Dates: With paring knife, make lengthwise slit in 1 pound pitted dates. Stuff each with about 1 teaspoon marzipan. Press a nut in center. Makes 55 to 60.

CARAMEL OATS

1/2	cup firmly packed brown sugar	1/4	cup margarine
1/2	cup Karo dark corn syrup	1	teaspoon salt
		6	cups round oat cereal
		1 1/2	cups peanuts

Grease 15 1/2 x 10 1/2 x 1-inch jelly roll pan. In 4-quart saucepan stirring constantly, heat brown sugar, corn syrup, margarine and salt over medium heat until margarine and sugar are melted. Remove from heat. Stir in cereal and nuts until well coated. Spread in prepared pan. Bake in 250°F oven 30 minutes, stirring frequently. Pour into greased large bowl; stir frequently about 10 minutes or until slightly cooled. Let stand about 1 hour. Store in tightly covered container. Makes about 8 cups.

BEVERAGES FOR ANY OCCASION

An amiable beverage, whether warm or cold, is an important companion to good eating or a pleasure to enjoy in itself. It may glisten with frost or glow with color. It may warm the spirit or cool the temper. And often as not, it may be made better for drinking with Karo corn syrup.

IMPERIAL PUNCH

3 cups water	4 oranges, peeled, sectioned
1 cup Karo light corn syrup	Juice of 6 lemons
1/2 teaspoon vanilla	1 bottle (750 ml) Rhine wine
1 small piece cinnamon stick	2 cups Kirsch liqueur
Peel from 1 lemon, sliced	1 bottle (750 ml) champagne, chilled
Peel from 1 orange, sliced	
1 can (13 1/2 oz) pineapple chunks in own juice	

In saucepan stir together water, corn syrup, vanilla, cinnamon stick, lemon and orange peel. Bring to boil over medium heat and boil 2 minutes. Cover; chill. Strain into punch bowl or large container. Add pineapple, orange sections, lemon juice, wine and Kirsch. Cover; chill several hours. Just before serving, add champagne. Makes 32 (1/2-cup) servings.

Top to bottom: *Strawberry Yogurt Milkshake*, p.113, *Peach Frost* p.113, *Hot Spiced Wine* p.109.

STRAWBERRY-TEA PUNCH

2 cups rosé wine
1 cup strong tea
1 cup Karo light
   corn syrup

1 cup orange juice
1 cup frozen
   strawberries

Place all ingredients in blender container; cover. Blend on high speed 15 seconds or until well mixed. Serve over ice in tall glasses. Garnish with orange slices. Makes 6 (1-cup) servings.

Tip: 1 cup fresh strawberries and 4 ice cubes may be substituted for frozen strawberries.

MERRY BERRY PUNCH

1 package (16 oz) frozen
   strawberries
1 can (6 oz) frozen
   orange juice
   concentrate
1 cup Karo light corn
   syrup

1 can (6 oz) frozen
   lemonade
   concentrate
1 bottle (32 oz) club
   soda, chilled

In blender container place 1/2 of the strawberries, orange juice and corn syrup; cover. Blend on high speed 30 seconds or until smooth. Add remaining strawberries and lemonade; cover. Blend well. Pour into punch bowl. Add club soda. Garnish with orange slices. Makes 16 (1/2-cup) servings.

FESTIVE SANGRIA

2 bottles (750 ml each)
   dry red wine, chilled
2 cups Karo light corn
   syrup
2 cups orange juice,
   chilled

1 cup lemon juice
2 bottles (12 oz each)
   club soda, chilled
2 oranges, sliced
1 lemon, sliced

In large punch bowl stir together wine, corn syrup, orange juice and lemon juice. Gradually mix in club soda. Add orange and lemon. Makes 26 (1/2-cup) servings.

RED WINE PUNCH

2 large lemons
2 bottles (750 ml each)
   dry red wine
2 cups Karo light corn
   syrup

1 bottle (32 oz) club
   soda, chilled

From center of lemons cut several thin slices; reserve. Into large bowl squeeze juice from remaining lemons. Stir in wine and corn syrup until well blended. Cover; chill. Just before serving, stir in club soda. Add ice. Garnish with reserved lemon slices. Makes 24 (1/2-cup) servings.

HOT SPICED WINE

4 cups water
1 1/2 cups Karo light corn
   syrup
1 cup raisins, divided
1/4 cup chopped candied
   ginger
4 (2-inch) cinnamon
   sticks

20 whole cloves
2 (3-inch) pieces orange
   peel
1 quart dry red wine
1 cup blanched whole
   almonds

In 3-quart saucepan bring water, corn syrup, 1/2 cup of the raisins, ginger, cinnamon sticks, cloves and orange peel to boil over medium heat. Reduce heat; simmer 45 minutes. Strain; discard spice mixture. Return corn syrup mixture to saucepan. Add wine. Heat until just heated through. (Do not boil.) Stir together remaining 1/2 cup raisins and nuts. Ladle hot mixture into 5-ounce punch cups. Add a heaping teaspoonful of raisin mixture to each cup. Serve immediately. Makes 12 (1/2-cup) servings.

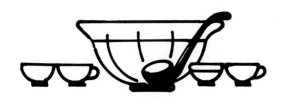

109

CITRUS WARMER

3 cups grapefruit juice	6 whole cloves
1/2 cup Karo light corn syrup	1 (3-inch) cinnamon stick
1/2 cup dark rum	

In 2-quart saucepan stir together all ingredients. Bring to boil over medium heat. Reduce heat and simmer 30 minutes. Remove cinnamon and cloves. Serve warm. Makes about 4 servings.

MULLED APPLE WINE

1 package (8 oz) dried apples	4 whole allspice
4 cups water	2 cups Karo light corn syrup
1/2 cup sugar	1 cup apple brandy
1 (3-inch) cinnamon stick	1 bottle (750 ml) dry white wine
1/4 teaspoon whole cloves	

In saucepan stir together apples, water, sugar, cinnamon stick, cloves and allspice. Bring to boil; reduce heat, cover and simmer 20 minutes. Pour into large container. Stir in corn syrup, brandy and wine. Cover and store in cool place at least 2 weeks. Remove spices. Keeps 1 month in refrigerator. Serve warm. Makes 2 1/2 quarts.

Tip: To revive a joyous tradition of the past, welcome a caroling party with steaming mugs of this warm, spicy wine.

IRISH COFFEE

1 1/2 ounces Irish whiskey	3/4 cup hot black coffee
2 tablespoons Karo light corn syrup	Whipped cream

In warmed coffee mug stir together whiskey and corn syrup. Add coffee. Top with whipped cream. Serve immediately. Makes 1 serving.

STRAWBERRY LIQUEUR

2 pints fully ripe strawberries, hulled, quartered	1 cup Karo light corn syrup
1 pint vodka	1/2 cup sugar

In large glass bowl stir together strawberries and vodka. Cover; refrigerate 5 days. In strainer placed over bowl place berries one layer at a time; press gently with back of spoon to let juices flow freely. Strain liquid through 6 layers of cheesecloth. Measure 3 cups. Add corn syrup and sugar. Stir until sugar is thoroughly dissolved. Pour into glass container. Cover tightly. Let stand 3 days to develop flavor. Makes 1 quart.

ALMOND LIQUEUR

1 cup Karo light corn syrup	1 1/2 tablespoons almond extract
1 cup sugar	1 teaspoon vanilla
1 pint vodka	1/2 cup whole almonds

In 1-quart saucepan stir together corn syrup and sugar. Stirring occasionally, bring to boil over medium heat. Remove from heat. Let stand 15 to 20 minutes. Stir in vodka. Stir in almond extract and vanilla. Pour into glass container. Add nuts. Cover tightly. Let stand 2 days to develop flavor. Makes about 1 quart.

Coffee Liqueur: Follow recipe for Almond Liqueur. Omit almond extract and almonds. Stir 3 tablespoons freeze-dried coffee into 3 tablespoons hot water. Add with vodka.

Orange Liqueur: Follow recipe for Almond Liqueur. Omit almond extract and almonds. Add 1 to 1 1/2 tablespoons orange extract and peel from 1 orange.

Chocolate Liqueur: Follow recipe for Almond Liqueur. Omit almond extract and almonds. Add 2 tablespoons chocolate extract.

Anise Liqueur: Follow recipe for Almond Liqueur. Omit almond extract and almonds. Add 2 teaspoons anise extract and peel from 1 lime.

HOLIDAY EGGNOG

6 eggs, separated	1/2 pint half-and-half
1/4 cup sugar	1/4 cup dark rum
1/2 cup Karo light corn syrup	1 pint vanilla ice cream
	Ground nutmeg

In large bowl with mixer at high speed beat egg whites until foamy. Gradually beat in sugar until stiff peaks form. In small bowl with mixer at medium-low speed beat egg yolks and corn syrup about 5 minutes or until thick and lemon colored. Add half-and-half. Beat until well mixed. Fold into egg white mixture. Stir in rum. Cover; chill. Place ice cream in one piece in punch bowl; pour eggnog over ice cream. Sprinkle with nutmeg. Makes 24 (1/2-cup) servings.

WATERMELON SMASH

3 cups pitted, diced watermelon	2 tablespoons lime juice
1/2 cup golden rum	2 teaspoons nonfat dry milk
1/4 cup Karo light corn syrup	6 ice cubes

Place all ingredients in blender container; cover. Blend on high speed 1 minute or until smooth. Makes 4 to 5 servings.

BANANA BASH

1 ripe banana, cut-up	1/4 cup lime juice
1/2 cup light rum	5 ice cubes, crushed
1/4 cup Karo light corn syrup	

In blender container place banana, rum, corn syrup and lime juice; cover. Blend on medium speed 30 seconds or until smooth. Add ice; blend 30 seconds. Garnish with lime slices. Makes 4 servings.

PEACH FROST

3 medium ripe peaches,
  pitted, peeled,
  quartered
1/2 cup Karo light corn
  syrup
1/4 teaspoon ground
  ginger

1 cup lemon sherbet
1/2 cup ginger ale
2 scoops vanilla ice
  cream

In blender container place peaches, corn syrup and ginger; cover. Blend on medium speed 30 seconds or just until smooth. Add sherbet and ginger ale; cover. Blend on medium speed 15 seconds or just until smooth. Pour into 2 large glasses. Top each with ice cream. Makes 2 servings.

STRAWBERRY YOGURT MILKSHAKE

1 1/2 cups strawberries,
  hulled
1 cup plain yogurt

1 cup skim milk
1/4 cup Karo light corn
  syrup

Place all ingredients in blender container; cover. Blend on high speed 2 minutes or until smooth and frothy. Makes 4 servings.

CHOCOLATE-BANANA SHAKE

1 pint chocolate ice
  cream
2 medium ripe bananas,
  cut-up

1/3 cup Karo light corn
  syrup
1/3 cup milk

Place all ingredients in blender container; cover. Blend on high speed 1 minute or until smooth and frothy. Makes 4 servings.

CANNING FOR THE FUTURE

Canning is a small investment in the future. In the past it was also a seasonal, and sometimes tedious, necessity. But, today, no-cook methods, perfected recipes, and convenience products such as Karo corn syrup, make canning a rewarding, uncomplicated and creative experience.

PEACH AND NECTARINE JAM

1 1/2	pounds ripe peaches	2	tablespoons lemon juice
1 1/2	pounds ripe nectarines	3 1/2	cups sugar
1	package (1 3/4 oz) powdered fruit pectin	1	cup Karo light corn syrup

Peel, pit and quarter peaches. Finely chop in food grinder, blender or processor. Measure 1 1/2 cups. Pit and quarter nectarines. Finely chop. Measure 1 1/2 cups. In 8-quart stainless steel or enamel saucepot stir together peaches, nectarines, pectin and lemon juice until well blended. Stirring constantly, bring to full rolling boil. Stir in sugar and corn syrup. Return to full rolling boil and stirring constantly, boil rapidly 1 minute. Remove from heat; skim surface. Immediately ladle into clean hot 1/2-pint jars leaving 1/4-inch headspace. Wipe top edge with damp towel. Seal according to jar manufacturer's directions. Process in boiling water bath 5 minutes. Cool jars on wire rack or folded towel. Makes about 6 (1/2-pint) jars.

Top to bottom: *Red Tomato Relish* p. 120,
Canned Dessert Pears p. 119, *Zucchini Pickle* p. 122,
No-Cook Peach Strawberry Jam p. 116.

NO-COOK PEACH STRAWBERRY JAM

1 1/2 pounds fully ripe peaches
1/4 teaspoon ascorbic acid crystals
1 pint strawberries
5 1/2 cups sugar

1 cup Karo light corn syrup
2 pouches (3 oz each) liquid fruit pectin
1/3 cup lemon juice

Peel, pit and thinly slice peaches. Crush peaches, one layer at a time, to let juice flow freely. Measure 1 3/4 cups. Stir in ascorbic acid. Hull strawberries; fully crush, one layer at a time, to let juice flow freely. Measure 1 cup. In large bowl stir together fruit, sugar and corn syrup until well blended. Let stand 10 minutes. In small bowl mix pectin and lemon juice. Stir into fruit mixture. Stir vigorously 3 minutes. Ladle into 1/2-pint freezer containers leaving 1/2-inch headspace (no paraffin needed). Cover with tight lids. Let stand at room temperature until set. (It may take up to 24 hours.) Jam to be eaten within a week or two may be stored in refrigerator. Freeze remaining containers; transfer to refrigerator as needed. Makes 8 (1/2-pint) containers.

Nectarine Jam: Follow recipe for No-Cook Peach Strawberry Jam. Substitute 2 1/4 pounds nectarines for peaches *and* strawberries. Increase ascorbic acid crystals to 1 teaspoon. Crush nectarines. Measure 2 3/4 cups.

Apricot Jam: Follow recipe for No-Cook Peach Strawberry Jam. Substitute 2 1/4 pounds apricots for peaches *and* strawberries. Crush apricots. Measure 2 3/4 cups.

NO-COOK PEACH RASPBERRY JAM

1 pound fully ripe peaches
1 1/2 cups fully ripe raspberries
3 cups sugar
1 cup Karo light corn syrup

1 pouch (3 oz) liquid fruit pectin
2 tablespoons lemon juice

Peel, pit and thinly slice peaches. Crush peaches, one layer at a time, to let juice flow freely. Measure 1 cup. Fully crush raspberries, one layer at a time, to let juice flow freely. Measure 1 cup. In large bowl stir together fruit, sugar and corn syrup until well blended. Let stand 10 minutes. In small bowl mix pectin and lemon juice. Stir into fruit mixture. Stir vigorously 3 minutes. Ladle into 1/2-pint freezer containers leaving 1/2-inch headspace (no paraffin needed). Cover with tight lids. Let stand at room temperature until set. (It may take up to 24 hours.) Jam to be eaten within a week or two may be stored in refrigerator. Freeze remaining containers; transfer to refrigerator as needed. Makes 5 (1/2-pint) containers.

Apricot Raspberry Jam: Follow recipe for No-Cook Peach Raspberry Jam. Substitute 1 pound fully ripe apricots for peaches.

Apricot Strawberry Jam: Follow recipe for No-Cook Peach Raspberry Jam. Substitute 1 pound fully ripe apricots for peaches and 1 pint fully ripe strawberries, hulled, for raspberries.

Strawberry Raspberry Jam: Follow recipe for No-Cook Peach Raspberry Jam. Substitute 1 pint fully ripe strawberries, hulled, for peaches. Fully crush strawberries. Measure 1 cup.

Raspberry Jam: Follow recipe for No-Cook Peach Raspberry Jam. Omit peaches. Use 3 cups fully ripe raspberries. Fully crush raspberries. Measure 2 cups.

Strawberry Jam: Follow recipe for No-Cook Peach Raspberry Jam. Substitute 1 quart fully ripe strawberries, hulled, for peaches *and* raspberries. Fully crush strawberries. Measure 1 3/4 cups. Increase pectin to 2 pouches (3 oz each).

RED PLUM JAM

3 pounds ripe red plums
2 cups sugar

2 cups Karo light corn syrup

Pit plums. Finely chop in food grinder, blender or processor. Measure 5 cups. In 6-quart stainless steel or enamel sauce-pot stir together plums, sugar and corn syrup. Let stand at room temperature 1 hour. Stirring constantly, bring to full rolling boil over high heat. Stirring occasionally, boil rapidly, 30 minutes or until mixture thickens*. (Stir frequently when mixture begins to thicken.) Remove from heat; skim surface. Immediately ladle into clean, hot 1/2-pint jars, leaving 1/4-inch headspace. Wipe top edge with damp towel. Seal according to jar manufacturer's directions. Process in boiling water bath 5 minutes. Cool jars on wire rack or folded towel. Makes about 4 (1/2-pint) jars.

*Pour small amount of boiling mixture on small cold plate. Place in freezer for a few minutes. If mixture gels, it is done.

AMBER MARMALADE

1 large grapefruit
1 large orange
1 large lemon
3 1/2 cups water

4 cups sugar
2 cups Karo light corn syrup

Remove peel from fruit; discard about one-half of the inner white part. With sharp knife, slice peel in very thin 1-inch long slivers. Section fruit and chop pulp. Place fruit pulp and peel (about 4 cups) in 8-quart stainless steel or enamel sauce-pot; add water. Stirring constantly, bring to full rolling boil. Stirring occasionally, boil gently 20 minutes. Add sugar and corn syrup. Stirring constantly, bring to full rolling boil over medium heat. Stirring occasionally, boil rapidly 60 minutes or until clear and thick. (Stir frequently when mixture begins to thicken.) Immediately ladle into clean, hot 1/2-pint jars, leaving 1/4-inch headspace. Wipe top edge with damp towel. Seal according to jar manufacturer's directions. Process in boiling water bath 10 minutes. Cool jars on wire rack or folded towel. Makes about 6 (1/2-pint) jars.

BLUEBERRY-STRAWBERRY JAM

3 pints strawberries
2 pints blueberries
3 cups sugar
1 1/2 cups Karo light corn syrup
1/2 cup lemon juice

Hull and crush strawberries. Measure 3 cups. Crush blueberries. Measure 3 cups. In 8-quart stainless steel or enamel saucepot stir together strawberries, blueberries, sugar, corn syrup and lemon juice. Stirring constantly, bring to full rolling boil. Stirring occasionally, boil rapidly 40 to 50 minutes or until mixture thickens (see p. 118). (Stir frequently when mixture begins to thicken.) Remove from heat; skim surface. Immediately ladle into clean, hot 1/2-pint jars, leaving 1/4-inch headspace. Wipe top edge with damp towel. Seal according to jar manufacturer's directions. Process in boiling water bath 5 minutes. Cool jars on wire rack or folded towel. Makes about 7 (1/2-pint) jars.

CANNED DESSERT PEARS

2 cups water
2 cups Karo light corn syrup
1/2 cup sugar
2 teaspoons vanilla
12 pounds firm ripe Bartlett pears (about 24)

In 8-quart stainless steel or enamel saucepot stir together water, corn syrup, sugar and vanilla. Stirring constantly, bring to boil and boil 5 minutes. Reduce heat and keep syrup warm. Peel, halve and core pears adding to syrup as soon as they are cut to prevent discoloring. Bring to boil and boil gently 5 minutes or until pears are tender. With slotted spoon immediately pack pears into clean hot 1-quart jars. Pour boiling syrup into jars completely covering pears and leaving 1/2-inch headspace. With non-metallic utensil release air bubbles. Seal according to jar manufacturer's directions. Process in boiling water bath 25 minutes. Cool jars on wire rack or folded towel. Makes about 3 (1-quart) jars.

PLUM CONSERVE

3 pounds ripe red plums	2 cups raisins
3 cups sugar	1 lemon, seeded, chopped
1 cup Karo light corn syrup	1 cup chopped walnuts

Pit plums. Finely chop in food grinder, blender or processor. Measure 5 cups. In 8-quart stainless steel or enamel saucepot stir together plums, sugar, corn syrup, raisins and lemon. Stirring constantly, bring to full rolling boil. Stirring occasionally, boil rapidly 50 minutes or until slightly thickened. (Stir frequently when mixture begins to thicken.) Stir in nuts. Immediately ladle into clean, hot 1/2-pint jars, leaving 1/4-inch headspace. Wipe top edge with damp towel. Seal according to jar manufacturer's directions. Process in boiling water bath 5 minutes. Cool jars on wire rack or folded towel. Makes about 8 (1/2-pint) jars.

RED TOMATO RELISH

2 cups coarsely chopped onion (1 lb)	1 cup sugar
1 cup diced sweet red pepper	2 tablespoons uniodized salt
1/2 cup diced green pepper	1 tablespoon dry mustard
3 pounds ripe tomatoes, peeled, coarsely chopped (6 cups)	2 teaspoons celery seed
2 cups white vinegar	1/2 teaspoon ground allspice
1 cup Karo light corn syrup	1/4 teaspoon crushed dried red pepper
	1 bay leaf

In 5-quart stainless steel or enamel saucepot stir together onion, pepper, tomatoes, vinegar, corn syrup, sugar, salt, mustard, celery seed, allspice, dried red pepper and bay leaf. Stirring constantly, bring to boil. Stirring occasionally, boil gently 1 hour. Immediately ladle into clean, hot 1/2-pint jars, leaving 1/4-inch headspace. Wipe top edge with damp towel. Seal according to jar manufacturer's directions. Process in boiling water bath 5 minutes. Cool jars on wire rack or folded towel. Makes about 5 (1/2-pint) jars.

MIXED VEGETABLE SWEET PICKLES

1 1/2 pounds small zucchini	2 cups Karo light corn syrup
1 1/2 cups sweet red pepper strips	2 cups white vinegar
1/4 cup uniodized salt	1 cup sugar
1 pound green beans	2 tablespoons mustard seed
2 cups thinly sliced carrots	2 (2 1/2-inch) cinnamon sticks, broken in half
3 cups water	
1 pound small white onions (about 11)	12 whole cloves
1 cup sliced celery	

Thinly slice zucchini. Measure 5 cups. In large bowl toss together zucchini, peppers and salt. Cover; let stand 8 hours or overnight. Drain; rinse 3 times in cold water. Drain; press to remove as much water as possible. Cut green beans in 1-inch pieces. Measure 3 cups. In 5-quart saucepot bring beans, carrots and water to boil over medium heat. Cover; boil 4 minutes. Add onions and celery; cover. Bring to boil; boil 5 minutes. Drain. Rinse in cold water; drain. In 5-quart stainless steel or enamel saucepot stir together corn syrup, vinegar, sugar, mustard seed, cinnamon and cloves. Stirring occasionally, bring to boil and boil 10 minutes. Add vegetables. Stirring frequently, bring to boil and boil 5 minutes. With slotted spoon immediately pack vegetables into clean, hot 1-pint jars. Pour boiling liquid into jars completely covering vegetables and leaving 1/4-inch headspace. Wipe top edge with damp towel. Seal according to jar manufacturer's directions. Process in boiling water bath 10 minutes. Cool jars on wire rack or folded towel. Makes about 4 (1-pint) jars.

BREAD AND BUTTER PICKLES

3 pounds unwaxed cucumbers	1 cup firmly packed brown sugar
3 1/2 cups thinly sliced onion	1 tablespoon mustard seed
1/4 cup uniodized salt	1 tablespoon celery seed
1 1/2 cups Karo light or dark corn syrup	1 tablespoon ground turmeric
1 1/2 cups cider vinegar	1/4 teaspoon pepper

Slice cucumbers 1/4-inch thick. Measure 9 cups. In large bowl toss together cucumbers, onion and salt. Cover; let stand 2 hours. Drain. Rinse with cold water; drain again. In 5-quart stainless steel or enamel saucepot stir together corn syrup, vinegar, sugar, mustard and celery seed, turmeric and pepper. Stirring constantly, bring to boil and boil 1 minute. Add vegetables. Bring to boil and boil 5 minutes. With slotted spoon immediately pack vegetables into clean, hot 1/2-pint jars. Pour boiling liquid into jars completely covering vegetables and leaving 1/4-inch headspace. Wipe top edge with damp towel. Seal according to jar manufacturer's directions. Process in boiling water bath 5 minutes. Cool jars on wire rack or folded towel. Makes about 4 (1-pint) jars.

ZUCCHINI PICKLE

3 pounds small zucchini	1 tablespoon mustard seed
1 1/2 cups thinly sliced onion	1 teaspoon celery seed
1/4 cup uniodized salt Water	1 teaspoon ground turmeric
2 cups cider vinegar	1/4 teaspoon dry mustard
1 1/2 cups sugar	
1 cup Karo light corn syrup	

Thinly slice zucchini. Measure 8 cups. In large bowl or stainless steel or enamel saucepot layer zucchini, onion, and salt. Cover with water. Let stand about 2 hours; drain. Rinse;

drain thoroughly. In 5-quart stainless steel or enamel sauce-pot, stir together vinegar, sugar, corn syrup, mustard and celery seed, turmeric and dry mustard. Bring to boil and boil 5 minutes. Add drained vegetables; immediately remove from heat. Mix well. Cover; let stand 2 hours. Stirring occasionally, bring to boil and boil 3 minutes. With slotted spoon immediately pack pickles into clean, hot 1/2-pint jars. Pour boiling liquid into jars completely covering pickles and leaving 1/4-inch headspace. Wipe top edge with damp towel. Seal according to jar manufacturer's directions. Process in boiling water bath 5 minutes. Cool jars on wire rack or folded towel. Makes about 8 (1/2-pint) jars.

GINGER PEAR CHUTNEY

4 pounds firm ripe pears, peeled, cored, diced (8 cups)	1/2 cup orange juice
	1 tablespoon grated lemon rind
1 pound onions, diced (3 cups)	1/4 cup lemon juice
1 1/2 cups Karo light corn syrup	1 teaspoon uniodized salt
1 1/2 cups cider vinegar	1 teaspoon ground ginger
1 cup firmly packed brown sugar	1/2 teaspoon ground allspice
1 cup raisins	
2 tablespoons grated orange rind	

In 5-quart stainless steel or enamel saucepot stir together pears, onions, corn syrup, vinegar, sugar, raisins, orange rind, orange juice, lemon rind, lemon juice, salt, ginger and allspice. Stirring constantly, bring to boil. Stirring occasionally, boil gently about 1 1/2 hours or until thickened (see p. 118). (Stir frequently when mixture begins to thicken.) Immediately ladle into clean, hot 1/2-pint jars, leaving 1/4-inch headspace. Wipe top edge with damp towel. Seal according to jar manufacturer's directions. Process in boiling water bath 5 minutes. Cool jars on wire rack or folded towel. Makes about 6 (1/2-pint) jars.

CUCUMBER MUSTARD PICKLES

2	quarts cold water	1/2	cup sugar
1/3	cup uniodized salt	1/4	cup unsifted flour
4	pounds unwaxed cucumbers, thinly sliced (12 cups)	1/4	cup dry mustard
		1	teaspoon ground turmeric
3 1/2	cups thinly sliced onion	2	cups cider vinegar
2	quarts boiling water	1	cup Karo light corn syrup

In large bowl stir together cold water and salt. Add cucumbers and onion. Cover; let stand 8 hours or overnight. Drain well. Cover vegetables with boiling water. Let stand 10 minutes; drain. In 5-quart stainless steel or enamel saucepot stir together sugar, flour, mustard and turmeric. Gradually stir in vinegar and corn syrup. Stirring constantly, bring to boil over medium heat and boil 2 minutes. Add vegetables. Stirring constantly, bring to boil. With slotted spoon immediately pack vegetables into clean, hot 1-pint jars. Pour boiling liquid into jars completely covering vegetables and leaving 1/4-inch headspace. Wipe top edge with damp towel. Seal according to jar manufacturer's directions. Process in boiling water bath 5 minutes. Cool jars on wire rack or folded towel. Makes about 5 (1-pint) jars.

TOMATO CHUTNEY

4	pounds ripe tomatoes	1	cup raisins
2	pounds apples	2	large cloves garlic, minced
1	pound onions, diced (3 cups)	1	tablespoon uniodized salt
2 1/2	cups diced sweet red pepper (2 lb)	1	tablespoon ground ginger
2	cups firmly packed brown sugar	1	teaspoon ground cinnamon
1 1/2	cups peeled, seeded, diced cucumbers (1 lb)	1/2	teaspoon ground allspice
1 1/2	cups Karo dark corn syrup	1/2	teaspoon ground coriander
1 1/2	cups cider vinegar		

Peel and cut tomatoes in chunks. Measure 7 cups. Peel, core and dice apples. Measure 5 1/2 cups. In 8-quart stainless steel or enamel saucepot stir together tomatoes, apples, onions, pepper, sugar, cucumbers, corn syrup, vinegar, raisins, garlic and salt. Stirring constantly, bring to boil. Stirring occasionally, boil gently 30 minutes. Stir in ginger, cinnamon, allspice and coriander. Stirring occasionally, continue boiling gently 1 hour or until thickened (see p. 118). (Stir frequently when mixture begins to thicken.) Immediately ladle into clean, hot 1/2-pint jars, leaving 1/4-inch headspace. Wipe top edge with damp towel. Seal according to jar manufacturer's directions. Process in boiling water bath 5 minutes. Cool jars on wire rack or folded towel. Makes 10 (1/2-pint) jars.

HAMBURGER RELISH

2 tablespoons mixed pickling spice	2 cups coarsely chopped green pepper
1 teaspoon whole cloves	1 cup diced sweet red pepper
1/4 teaspoon crushed dried red pepper (optional)	2 cups cider vinegar
2 (2 1/2-inch) cinnamon sticks, broken in half	1 cup Karo light corn syrup
4 pounds ripe tomatoes, peeled, coarsely chopped (7 cups)	1 cup firmly packed brown sugar
1 pound onions, coarsely chopped (3 cups)	1 tablespoon uniodized salt

Tie pickling spice, cloves, dried red pepper and cinnamon in cheesecloth to make spicebag. In 5-quart stainless steel or enamel saucepot stir together spicebag, tomatoes, onions, pepper, vinegar, corn syrup, sugar and salt. Stirring constantly, bring to boil. Stirring frequently, boil gently about 1 1/2 hours. Remove spicebag. Immediately ladle into clean, hot 1/2-pint jars, leaving 1/4-inch headspace. Wipe top edge with damp towel. Seal according to jar manufacturer's directions. Process in boiling water bath 5 minutes. Cool jars on wire rack or folded towel. Makes about 5 (1/2-pint) jars.

Index

Main Dishes

Beef

Frankfurters

Lamb

Pork

Poultry

Sauces and Glazes

Seafood

Vegetables

Salads